Living in Purpose

On Your Way to A Greater Identity in Christ

Brenda Murphy

Scripture quotations taken from the Amplified® Bible (AMP), Copyright © 2015 by The Lockman Foundation Used by permission. www.Lockman.org

The Holy Bible, Berean Study Bible, BSB Copyright ©2016, 2018 by Bible Hub Used by Permission. All Rights Reserved Worldwide.

Scripture quotations marked CSB®, are taken from the Christian Standard Bible®, Copyright© 2017 by Holman Bible Publishers. Used by permission. Christian Standard Bible®, and CSB® are federally registered trademarks of Holman Bible Publishers.

"Scripture quotations marked (ESV) are taken from The ESV® Bible (The Holy Bible, English Standard Version®), copyright © 2001 by Crossway, a publishing ministry of Good News Publishers. Used by permission. All rights reserved."

Scripture quotations marked (KJV) are from The Authorized (King James) Version. Rights in the Authorized Version in the United Kingdom are vested in the Crown. Reproduced by permission of the Crown's patentee, Cambridge University Press

Scripture quotations marked MSG are taken from THE MESSAGE, copyright © 1993, 1994, 1995, 1996, 2000, 2001, 2002 by Eugene H. Peterson. Used by permission of NavPress. All rights reserved. Represented by Tyndale House Publishers, Inc.

Scripture quotations taken from the New American Standard Bible® (NASB), Copyright © 1960, 1962, 1963, 1968, 1971, 1972, 1973, 1975, 1977, 1995 by The Lockman Foundation , Used by permission. www.Lockman.org

Scripture quotations marked (NIV) are taken from the Holy Bible, New International Version®, NIV®. Copyright © 1973, 1978, 1984, 2011 by Biblica, Inc.™ Used by permission of Zondervan. All rights reserved worldwide. www.zondervan.com The "NIV" and "New International Version" are trademarks registered in the United States Patent and Trademark Office by Biblica, Inc.™

Living in Purpose

Scriptures marked (NKJV) are taken from the New King James Version®. Copyright © 1982 by Thomas Nelson. Used by permission. All rights reserved.

Scripture quotations marked (NLT) are taken from the Holy Bible, New Living Translation, copyright ©1996, 2004, 2015 by Tyndale House Foundation. Used by permission of Tyndale House Publishers, Inc., Carol Stream, Illinois 60188. All rights reserved.

Cover design by Rick Schroeppel, Elm Street Design Studio.

Copyright © 2018 Brenda Murphy

All rights reserved. No part of this book may be reproduced in any form or by any electronic or mechanical means, including information storage and retrieval systems, without permission in writing from the publisher, except by reviewers, who may quote brief passages in a review or quotes within the limits of the Fair Use Act.

Publisher: bylisabell
Radical Women
(DBA)
PO Box 782
Granbury, TX
76048
www.bylisabell.com

ISBN-10: 1-7325363-3-3
ISBN-13: 978-1-7325363-3-3

We are assured and know that [God being a partner in their labor] all things work together and are [fitting into a plan] for good to and for those who love God and are called according to [His] design and purpose.

Romans 8: 28 (AMP)

This book is dedicated to my sisters, both naturally speaking as well as spiritually so. They are the women who have supported me, challenged me, and encouraged me throughout my personal journey.

At times, my sisters can be counted upon to provide for me in both word and in deed, moral support, trust and feedback that has proven to be both beneficial as well as empowering.

Your love, time, endurance, and generosity will never be forgotten. Thank you for helping me to soar to higher heights and deeper depths so I can reach my greatest potential in life, which is to leave a meaningful purposeful legacy for others to know we indeed serve an Awesome God!

Brenda Murphy

"The only impossible journey is the one you never begin."
                    ~ Anthony Robbins

Table of Contents

ACKNOWLEDGMENTS i

Section One ....

   I. Epiphany 1

   II. Purpose through the Eyes of Another 4

   III. In the Beginning—Finding my Way 18

   IV. You Call Me Lord—May I Call You Servant? 24

   V. My Greatest Strength Was Proven In My Smallest Test 39

Section Two ....

   VI. It Ain't What it Looks Like 60

   VII. Don't Expect a Crowd to Attend 67

   VIII. Wait On Him, He Will Deliver on Time 75

   IX. Comfort in His Name 79

Section Three ....

   X. Soul Caretaker 88

   XI. His Purpose is in His Promise 99

   XII. He is a Mighty Good Leader 108

   XIII. After You Go Through, There's No Way Out But Up. 114

Section Four ....

   XIV. When Your Trial Becomes Your Greatest Test-I-mony 122

XV. All Things Are Working For My Good 137

XVI. This Too Shall Pass 138

XVII. A Yet Praise! 145

XVIII. You Should not Follow Who You Don't Know 152

XIX. A Final Note Regarding Purpose 158

References 176

ABOUT THE AUTHOR 177

Other Books Published By Brenda Murphy 179

ACKNOWLEDGMENTS

I would like to thank the Mastermind behind the inspiring book cover for *Living in Purpose*, Rick Schroeppel. Through your encouraging words of creativity and artwork, I was challenged to explore and express my creative side to imagining what *Living in Purpose* revealed to me on the outside.

I would also like to personally thank my editor and publisher, Lisa Bell, for the generosity of her time, talent, skill, prayers and support in the completion of my new book and fourth book, *Living in Purpose*. Your dedication, desire and commitment to me during this entire process to bring out the best in me and my work is priceless, and I am forever grateful for your coaching and encouragement.

To Bishop Gary Oliver, your ability to lead by example, guide and support others as we learn and grow in the knowledge of Christ has ignited a spiritual hunger within me to ask for more and to anticipate greater expectation in my personal relationship with God. My family and I are so blessed to be a part of the Family of Tabernacle of Praise where the liberty of true praise has free reign!

Brenda Murphy

SECTION ONE

"For I know the plans I have for you," declares the LORD, "plans to prosper you and not to harm you, plans to give you hope and a future."

Jeremiah 29:11 (NIV)

I. EPIPHANY

For years, I searched endlessly for answers outside the scope and full understanding of what the Word of God said I was created to be. At times, I allowed my life to be aligned or patterned with what I saw others I admired say and do rather than hold fast and true to what God's word said I am.

After years of chasing at times a miscued thought and not so clear vision of how God saw me through His precious lenses, I arrived at one conclusion—it had all been for naught. And in certain limited occasions, personal dead ends of fulfillment and disillusion about where I possibly went wrong in the purpose and pursuit for my life.

Thankfully one day, while in prayer and reading the Word of God, I came to the understanding that I am the purpose, and I am also on purpose, through the assignment of God's divine purpose that He placed upon my life to carry out His specific will in the earth.

Now, before I could truly bask in my new revelation of this word, I realized I needed to search further into what exactly this exposure really meant to me. This need lead me back up to Jeremiah 29:7. *"Seek the peace and the prosperity of the city to which I have carried you into exile. Pray to the Lord for it, because if it prospers, you too will prosper."* (NIV)

Before the prophet shares this promise, he must give them a directive from God, which was to seek the peace and prosperity of the city in which they currently lived. They were considered to be in exile (refugee or an outcast).

The Israelites, much like us today, did not want to hear this message at all! They wanted to be greeted with and at the very least told they were going home. They wanted to be told their suffering was going to end—not only soon but perhaps at that moment.

To their amazement, that was not God's plan at all. Instead, God's plan was for them to stay right where they were and help prosper the nation (are you ready for this?) that enslaved them in the first place. If you think that was something, wait for it.

The next biggest shock of their lives came in verse 10 of Jeremiah. *"For thus said the LORD, that after seventy years be accomplished at Babylon I will visit you, and perform my good word toward you, in causing you to return to this place."* (NIV)

This meant none in the current generation of Israelites would be returning to their homes until they were old. Some would never see their homeland again. You can only imagine what a crushing, disappointing blow they felt from Jeremiah's words.

We believe God knows the plans He has for us. Ultimately He will give us a splendid future. However, it is important that we understand and accept the fact that as we walk out our challenging and sometimes difficult lives on this earth, we must remember—the best growth comes from persevering through our trials, and not escaping them entirely.

It is by our understanding of perseverance through various trials, we find in the end, an unspeakable joy that could not and may not have been fulfilled through any other means or method.

Today, search your heart and mind and discover what hard or difficult thing you are currently going through. Consider while you may be in the midst of this suffering, you too can choose to cling to Jeremiah 29:11. But be willing to cling to it for the right reasons.

Don't cling because you want to believe God is going to take away all of your suffering, heartaches, pains, and challenges and give you an easy, non-challenging journey or a life filled with carefree smoothness. It won't happen.

Choose to live in the truth—gospel confidence He will give you hope in the midst of your trials, heartache, pain, suffering, misunderstanding, lack, fear and doubts.

"Your word is a lamp to my feet and a light to my path."

Psalm 119:105 (AMP)

II. PURPOSE THROUGH THE EYES OF ANOTHER

Intentional, deliberate, persistent, perseverance, tenacity, resolve determination and drive are just a few synonyms that come to mind when I think about the word purpose.

Purpose is such a powerful and definite word. Purpose is a word of intent. When spoken, there is no question about its origin. It is a word or a phrase simply meant to imply "be." No guess work. No oversight. No happenstance or mishap. The intent was done, well, purposefully.

The word purpose according to Webster's Revised Unabridged Dictionary is a noun meaning "that which a person sets before himself as an object to be reached or accomplished; the end or aim to which the view is directed in any plan, measure, or exertion; view; aim; design; intention; plan." In other words, the word "purpose" could also be looked at as being "a deliberate set-up."

For me, understanding I was not birthed into the world without a just cause and reasoning but that I was intended by God is breathtaking. Praise God, no matter what it looked like, I was meant to be here in time, space and purpose.

I choose to bless God because I didn't arrive too soon, too late, ahead of scheduled or prematurely. I was envisioned by God to arrive in the earth on time and in God's own divine timing and will for my divine assignment!

I was anticipated to arrive on the scene of my life at my appointed time, set by the hands of an Almighty God in my "purpose." I didn't have to wait to be assigned work by a committee of sorts. I didn't have to be outfitted into or around someone else's agenda or at their discretion.

God, had already preassigned my destiny and formed me for the work at hand prior to my delivery. He fortified me, strengthened me, approved of me, anointed me, chose me and appointed me for such a time as now.

I remember at an early age, I did not know how to define myself as it relates to purpose. Neither did I possess the wherewithal or the sense of belonging and what any of that meant for me.

Admittedly, without that knowledge of understanding, I was left with a sense of emptiness and incompletion. No matter what I had accomplished at a young age, I was always left with a feeling of there must be something more.

In my early childhood, there was never any shortage of criticism from individuals who felt the need to critique my life on what they felt I didn't have as a skillset or even the ability to accomplish anything in my life. At least not from their viewpoint.

At times, there were those who could not wait to infer I would never amount to anything or that my personal dreams and aspirations were entirely too vast for me to remotely succeed. Often they implied that perhaps I should scale down a bit so as not to be disappointed should they not come true. Some felt I was getting my hopes up for a tremendous let down.

Nevertheless, I still felt compelled to dream and believe that one day my life would come full circle, and it would have incredible purpose and realness. I chose to keep dreaming because the dreams were never farfetched to me. In fact, the more I dreamed, the more I felt they were not just merely dreams. My realities simply waited to be sculpted into God's perfect plan and will for my life.

I never doubted one day my dreams would be manifested into purpose. They were not just out there somewhere in outer space with a mystical unoccupied intent. I believed the things I saw in my thoughts and hopes were not just some magical young child's fairy tale she hoped might someday come true. My joy was full of hope in possibilities.

I knew and believed deeply that God was on my side. No matter what I had to endure, I could still have the audacity to hope and believe God would one day see me through, and He alone would allow me to receive the very dreams I prayed for.

To this day, I kept on believing my dreams were possible, achievable and conceivable and one day they would become my reality. All I have ever lived and breathed for was to do the will of God wholeheartedly. Nothing else filled my heart like that possibility.

I loved the name of Jesus on my lips and in my heart. Even being young at the time, I was smitten and captured with His very presence in my thought life. For as long as I can remember, saying His name gave me an instantaneous jolt of energy, vitality, hope and life.

For many, many hours I would sit and daydream about how I might be used for building up the Kingdom. I would search for everything I could possibly get my hands on to read about the Word of God and how I might receive more and more of His presence into my life.

As a born again believer, I could sense I had every right

to be a part of God's perfect plan and the freedom to expand and explore all the unlimited possibilities He had for my life.

I was afraid to fly naturally speaking. However, in my dreams, there were no boundaries, restrictions or fear. I was being made free to soar to unlimited levels and intervals with God — to great levels and heights as I choose to believe.

At the age of nine, when God saved me, I believed even then I was free to roam about the earth and trust God for what I pleased. If I had indeed found favor in His sight, no weapon forming itself against me would prosper or cause me never to accomplish that plan for my life.

Once I started dreaming, I never stopped, nor did I have any desire to stop. When I dreamed, my hopes, thoughts and prayers would transport me far above what the world classifies as being normal or realistic. Even today, my dreams take me to great places of wealth, privilege, righteousness and prosperity in God and places of ability and personal responsibility.

When I dream, I am not bound by naysayers, haters, or prejudices. I am free to be as God anointed me to be. I am delivered from the negative stigmas of this world and the confining thoughts of this limited domain.

I choose to believe I am worthy in the eyes of God. I stand before Him in my dreams, as pure and righteous through the shed blood upon the Cross at Calvary. So I live in my dreams day and night, because they minister to me and guide me through life's roughness and at times rude and harsh awareness.

From the time of my youth, I truly believed I had something noteworthy about what Jesus had done in my personal life to share with the world. I wanted to share how God healed my body and was keeping me from day to day. All I knew was the more He blessed my young life, I needed to tell others about Him in the only manner I knew.

I chose to believe to keep trusting God and asking Him to please show me the steps and order for my young life. I wanted more. I craved more. I needed more from Him, and the more I sought after Him, His presence covered me, at times hovering over me. Even still, the dreams and the longing for Him kept coming.

I discovered in my pursuit of God, the more I went after him, the more I detected a strong sense of His drawing me closer to Him—to run after His voice and His presence in my life. I certainly did not understand most of this process. I just knew it was compelling me to follow Him, so I did. And I have never had any desire to look back, or even remotely go back ever since.

Nevertheless, during my early childhood, I continued to make my longing known to everyone who would listen. I would talk often about my love for Jesus and my hope to serve Him always.

Funny now—not so much then—half the kids my age often laughed and called me names, saying I was weird. Perhaps I was to them. However, I knew I loved God, and I wanted more of our time spent together, no matter the cost.

As I continued to grow in the Lord, I was persistent in prayer, because I did not fully understand a lot. Rather than ask others who probably wouldn't have known either or just thought I was strange, I decided to talk to God directly, and in my own words, tell Him how I truly felt. I saw my mother do the same thing on many, many occasions.

Often I witnessed Mother talking to God on several weekly discussions about everything. I used to think "Who is she talking too so much?" I noticed when she entered into the presence of God, she seemed totally at home there. She wasn't hurried, bothered, stressed or worried about time.

She just entered in at ease and stayed as long as she cared to.

My mother didn't try to hide her feelings or emotions when it came to prayer. She just started talking and before she knew it, her hands were wailing in the air, tears rolling down her face. Anyone remotely near her could readily feel the presence of what she described as being in His peace all around her.

I watched as those hands went up in the air, and yes, you guessed it. Right there where she stood, out of her mouth, went a tremendous praise and worship from her lips.

What I readily admired about my mother was her freedom to worship deliberately. There was no specific formula, rhyme or reasoning for her. She wasn't bothered by onlookers who might wonder "What in the world is she doing?"

Some people may have criticized her unusual method of worship, which I lovingly call "free-styling," meaning my mother constantly sung around the house, in the car, while cooking, in the yard, at church or wherever she felt the need for worship.

To me, it appeared to be some sort of release for her to do so. She looked more relaxed and assured that all was well or at least had the potential to be so. Honestly, I believed my mother was in a class all on her own during those special moments, and nothing else truly mattered. What I admired most about her was she seemed to have a pulse on what mattered to her — to get what she needed from God. And she went after it with everything in her.

I saw my mother give God praise on any and all occasions. Happy, sad, mad, angry, stressed, distressed, disappointed, triumphant or when she felt defeated. Still she worshipped. Now I realized she wasn't praising because she felt those things. She was praising because who God was to her while being immersed in those things.

On many occasions, she would tell me, "You must always trust God for everything."

And those moments stayed with me even to this day. I will never forget what an impact her praise and worship lifestyle did for my life. It opened my eyes in a whole lot of ways. It completely molded and shaped the entire journey I am on right now.

"Why?" you may ask. Because I knew early on, her worship was for real. Nothing fake about it. It wasn't pretentious at all. It wasn't over the top or too dramatic. It was simply and fully from her heart.

She gave God open praise at every conceivable moment she thought of His goodness and His greatness to her life — especially when it involved her beloved family, which meant everything to my mother. Her children undoubtedly were her total pride and joy.

Even as a young girl, I also witnessed firsthand God openly rewarding my mother on several occasions. I believed He did so because of her openness and her willingness to serve Him with all she had. She had intensity for His presence. My mother had the kind of God favor that made others envious or at the very least, made her blush.

There were times, I promise you, it looked as though my mother had this secret weapon through her prayer life and praise that caused heaven to respond to her immediate needs in many specific incidents, even when the outside of her world looked dense at best.

To the outside world, I am sure my mother's lifestyle to others may not have appeared to be much, at least not enough for her to seriously relish with such tremendous praise as she often displayed. What they didn't know was on the inside of her, she knew who was in control of her life and that of her entire family.

She had a meaningful, respectful and deliberate relationship with her Lord and Savior. Most of all, she knew how to render unto God what was spiritually due and righteous to His name. She knew how to hold a conversation with God like nobody's business.

I did not know exactly what to make of all this. Nevertheless, I continued to watch and admire her from afar.

Because I loved my mother dearly, I would pray continuously, "Lord, I want to be just like my mother, especially in her prayer life with you when I grow up. God, when I grow up, please allow me to worship as I see her praise you. And I want to know you for real."

My mother did not have any particular or special method she used when she prayed. She talked to Him with her daily dialogue as though she was speaking with a close and familiar friend. Sometimes it was out loud through a, "Lord, have mercy praise." Or "thank you Jesus over and over again."

It wasn't even how she said it, but more or less what she did with it through her worship. She worshipped in true conviction. Her God was truly worthy of "her praise." Morning, noon or night, in her opinion, He alone was worthy of all she was.

Times were extremely difficult for my mother and father to raise their family of 10 children. Their limited income and even lesser education between the two of them stretched them constantly. Sometimes, their days were met with much noticeable challenges than anyone could see from miles away. However, together, my parents complemented each other well through their strong faith in God and their visible respect and love for each other.

When one showed visible signs of weakness, the other declared victory and encouraged the other. Inevitably they both conceded God was their victor in it all.

They depended on each other for natural strength, and when they had disagreements, my dad was always the one who would relent first and simply walk away or laugh out loud at my mother. His actions didn't always make her smile, but she knew he loved her anyway.

Together, what they lacked in education, God made up for with their incredible, undeniable, earthshattering faith and belief. When every earthly odd was stacked up against them, they still believed God, and they communicated with Him daily in their own special way. No matter what came against them, they stood on one accord and love. They prayed and helped each other through the toughest of times.

Mom through her open prayers and uplifted hands, and Dad through his singing and constant parables. I don't know if they really grasped what they were doing in the natural realm during those difficult times, Even though I wasn't quite sure either, thankfully, I watched and payed close attention to pretty much every detail.

If anyone cared to know my take on the observation, I would call it leaving a legacy for their children and grandchildren to remember just how good God is long after they were called home to be with the Lord. My, how we as a family benefited from that concept.

Today I realized the word purpose has very little to do with the individual or the role being played. It has everything to do with the fact of who is really in control of our destiny.

I felt my parents had this secret that was really greater than they fully understood or spiritually comprehended.

They looked at life through a whole different set of lenses. They believed God was just God all by Himself, and with Him, there were no boundaries or limitations.

They didn't raise their family with a lot of amenities or extravagant gifts or gadgets. They didn't have a lot of flamboyant things to offer each or any of the children to be quite honest. They certainly could not afford to make promises they could not live up to or keep.

But even in the midst of what often appeared to be a no way out lifestyle or situation, they somehow really believed there was a God looking out for them. And He cared about them and would bring them through not in the "nick" of time, but every time.

I watched my mother on many occasions, multitask like nobody's business. She could do her church duties and still be aware of what child was where and doing whatever. She could be in the kitchen cooking and at the same time assign everyone a specific chore to handle to completion. And don't even think about asking her how soon it needed to be completed. We had no chance to put off obedience.

I remember her trade phrase would be something like, "Don't worry about it. Just have it done by the time I get back."

To me, that spelled the word "F-E-A-R" in layman's terms. She was a wife, mother, sister, aunt, niece and a wonderful nurturer all at the same time—sometimes all of the above in one day.

She gave most often out of her resolve and insufficiency. I am convinced there were multiple times she put her children and husband first before her own needs were ever considered, let alone met. Her family meant the absolute world to her.

I believe she understood her family was one of the most

precious gifts ever given to her by God Himself. She simply adored each of us. Oh yeah she fussed, put each of us in our rightful places, and would let each of us know when we were out of place and how to slide back into it in a hurry.

All of my parent's lives, one of the most important lessons I learned from them both was it really mattered to them how they lived their lives before others and their community. They took their walk with Christ with total reverence and respect for the name of Jesus.

Realizing now the word perfect does not mean flawless or without mistakes. Both my parents lived their lives forever growing and learning in the wisdom and knowledge that there was something or someone much, much greater than themselves.

And they looked to Him for constant guidance, help and deliverance. Crisis or no crisis, they prayed. Food on the table or not, they prayed. Children sick or healthy as a horse, still they prayed for the blood covering of Jesus to reign over their household.

And when there was no money to take their children or themselves to the hospital, my parents used home remedies. Still they prayed, laid hands on us and trusted God for the best outcome, and God did just that.

They were relentless in their pursuit after God, and they admonished everyone who came into contact with them to do the same. Down through the years some folk classified them as being "old." I classified them as being "relevant" for the kingdom.

They had a true reverent fear and love for God. One that was always noticeable and on display without trying to be, which added to their daily testament that our God is indeed worthy of all the praise. Not everyone will love you and celebrate you or the Christ that lives in you, but my parents never thought twice about not trusting God or allowing their God-given light to shine brightly everywhere they went.

As I continue to grow today in my adult life, from time to time, I find myself reminiscing about what some may call "the good old days." I cannot help but believe what I was witnessing first hand back then, would be defined today as purpose unfolding right before my very eyes. My parents simply lived it out loud before the world at large.

I describe purpose as being a specific assignment appointed by God for my life, given to me before birth that only I can accomplish through the power, grace and mercies of God. Purpose is the assignment attached to my identity while I am here on this earth.

I am privileged, through my daily living, open communication and every day walking my life out before the world, to be a living, viable, energetic instrument for kingdom building.

While praying things through and finishing that which God alone has assigned me to do in His name, I am careful to pay attention to the people and things around me to make sure I am doing it God's way and not with my own agenda.

Within the particular scope of the purpose for my life, I have been given the ability, wisdom, strength, power, and the anointing to run in my purpose while being able to complete those particular tasks or assignments given for me to do. I know and am fully persuaded according to Isaiah 54:17

> *"No weapon formed against you shall prosper,*
> *And every tongue which rises against you in judgment*
> *You shall condemn.*
> *This is the heritage of the servants of the LORD,*
> *and their righteousness is from Me,"*

says the LORD. (NKJV)

I understand the purpose for my life's journey will not be accomplished without determination, persistence, perseverance, drive and resolution. I realize without the aide and assistance of the Holy Spirit and the Lord ordering my steps, the full potential and purpose for my life will never materialize. It will never be fully released by simply sitting on the sidelines being content or through wishful thinking.

Even though God has assigned purpose to my life, I am aware there will be proverbial strongholds vying at every single turn to try to deter, detain, destroy and even delay me from reaching the goal for my journey. However, coming into immediate agreement with God daily and acknowledging Him in all of my ways is the only way I can justifiably make it.

I have learned I am nothing without the presence of God in my walk. And the more I choose to rest in Him and seek His direction for my life, the more progress I am able to make.

Purpose also lets me know God deliberately and intentionally allowed me to be birthed into the earthly realm despite the hardship and many adjustments my parents faced. They were poor people with a prayer and a plan, and they chose to believe God and deliberately hang on to the promise that tomorrow would be better for them and their unborn children.

God alone knew the child they carried had a purpose for the planet and for His good pleasure and the benefit of helping others. I am so excited God loved me into His specific plan and place for my spiritual purpose. He carefully meted out the blueprint, scoping out every intricate detail and design for His daily usage of my being.

Everything about me means something special to Him.

From my unique footprint to the very strands of hair on my head says, "Details in progress."

Whereas I use to be extremely nervous about every little mishap and mistake I made fearing I would somehow fall out of the perfect will and plan of God. Now, I am learning to relax and understand, it's okay, because according to God's manual, I am still under construction. And He alone still approves of me right where I am.

Through purpose, I recognize the need for humbleness, gratitude and gratefulness. All glory and honor is due the name of Jesus because of His plan He has in store for my personal journey.

Waking up each morning, *"Being confident of this, that he who began a good work in you will carry it on to completion until the day of Christ Jesus."* [Philippians 1:6 (NIV)] makes me smile, eager to do His appointed will for my life all over again.

> *"The steps of a good man are ordered by the LORD: and he delighteth in his way."*
>
> Psalm 37:23 (KJV)

III. IN THE BEGINNING—FINDING MY WAY

As long as I can remember being in this world, I can remember dreaming big. It didn't really matter to me at the moment whether or not I possessed all the particulars to accomplish the goals at the time. I just had an "I believe wild card in my stomach" that somehow and some way, I would prevail in the process. I remember always setting minimum, tangible goals and believed God for the potential to reach and perhaps even exceed them in due season.

I cannot think of a single day ever going by that I didn't visualize myself being successful in whatever I put my hands to do. Call me crazy, but I simply chose to believe God. Even though I cannot physically see Him, I still choose to believe God for everything. When I didn't have much in the natural realm, I saw big and incredible things possible for my immediate future in the spiritual realm.

I felt it. I sensed in my spiritual eyes mind through my faith that I was placed here on earth for something greater than my vocabulary or my personal strength and ability at the time would be able to deliver. While some may describe it as being "potential," I simply identify it today as being

God's purpose flowing through my spiritual veins.

Still, it didn't really matter. I believed and dared to dream big. Growing up like most homes and families back in the day, if you had what was considered as the daily "necessities," which was food, clothes and shelter, you were considered blessed beyond measure.

Thankful I had a praying mother and a hands on dad at all times, along with five brothers and four sisters, a portion of good health and strength, I called myself blessed and highly favored!

There was no such thing as being bored or lazy in our household because activities were the name of the game — cleaning up the house, feeding the animals or just merely staying out of trouble. Entertainment meant playing activities outside or preparing to complete homework or chores on the inside as a kid. If you had parents like mine, their number one goal, it seemed, was to make sure kids were always preoccupied doing something positive. After all, "An idle mind was the devil's workshop." At least that's what I was always told. Nevertheless, being creative and productive were my two favorite adjectives, because to some degree, it meant I had some say-so in the matter at hand. And off I went to discover the world at large with my vision board in tow.

In my neighborhood, I was always the group's leader. I was always coming up with activities and ideas to put into place. I absolutely loved being the leader, and putting all the pieces together was a no-brainer activity for me.

I actually lived and breathed "opportunity" to express my creativity. Planning an event was something I could readily do in my sleep with minimum preparation, and I loved every single moment of it.

Equally, I enjoyed being a blessing to others and helping

others reach their greatest potential even when I was the same age as the next kid. Doing this brought me my greatest joy. It has only increased in adulthood for me even until this very day. Nothing much in this particular area has changed.

I honestly believe I was born to serve and assist others. To help birth into their lives their greatest probable goal and dreams and aide them in finishing their personal race, no matter how challenging or difficult it appears to be.

To this day, when I see a need, great or small, I literally get an adrenaline rush to come to the aide and assistance of that individual and support when I believe God leads me to do so. I enjoy helping those who are really and truly seeking the will of God for their lives.

However, responding in such a manner did not always meet with great return from others. Not everyone was necessarily receptive or delighted by my efforts in trying to accentuate the positive in the lives of others around me or themselves.

I had to learn what, when and how along the way — when to step in and offer assistance and when to walk away. When it was not wanted or warranted. I also had to learn to not become offended otherwise. I always liked the Kenny Rogers song, "The Gambler." You have to know when to hold onto your cards and when to throw them down. Like he expressed, you might need to walk away from the game, and sometimes even run. And when the dealin' is done, you can finally count your winnings.

I understand everyone has a special gift given to them by God. Without a doubt, I knew from a very young age, one of my gifts was in the realm of encouragement. I live and breathe to motivate. I am empowered to encourage others in every way I can.

In fact, being close to my mother, she often said to me,

"Never say what you will and won't do." While I now understand what she meant by that statement; there was always a big part of me that knew exactly what strengths I had and where my limitations and cutoff points were. Even in that knowledge, I still have a pressing desire not to allow my weaknesses to overshadow the positive.

At an early age, I knew I was destined for greatness. I wasn't sure how it was all going to unfold, but I never had any real doubt the greatness in me would one day take place in my life in a major and explosive manner. I released the fact that at God's appointed time, and when each opportunity presented itself, I was moving forward without any doubts or hesitations.

I was born again in the Lord at the young age of nine years old. Accepting Jesus Christ into my life literally changed me forever. It wasn't just the water baptism or the attending of church services Wednesdays and Sundays or the typical Bible studies, vocational Bible studies (VBS) or Baptist Training Union (BTU) meetings and activities alone. But for me, it was all about applying the personal life applications in the moments that made all the difference in the world to me.

It's difficult to put a pulse on it, but I knew I craved more for my daily walk with God. I sensed I was created for more. Daily, my relationship with God required of me more of His attention, His presence and His guidance. I longed for deeper depths of His presence in my life.

The additional dialogue I had with Him made me feel more sustained, assured and secured. Just having a mere run in with Him every now and then was not enough. I needed Him. I longed for Him. I searched desperately for Him. I actually wanted a "relationship" with Him.

My daily conversations with God always left me feeling

I was still dwelling in His presence long after the verbal communicating from my lips ended. Even when I stopped talking to Him, He was always constantly in my thoughts.

Being in the presence of God left me with a feeling of being energized and vibrant. Even though I did not always care to share my innermost thoughts with others my age or older, I felt totally relaxed and at home sharing my heart with Him alone. I trusted Jesus with my life and everything in between.

Somehow, whatever I chose to share with Him left an assurance that He was really listening and cared about what I had to say. Even though I was just a kid in the beginning of our relationship, every moment spent in His presence was a priceless treasure to me.

I felt wiser and more secure, as if I had been privileged to receive knowledge I shouldn't have otherwise had access to. During my quiet time in the presence of God, I never thought it strange or uncomfortable, because I didn't share this part of my life with others. It was my private time alone, and I cherished every moment of it.

Fast forwarding to my life today — as an adult, I still feel this way except with more intensity. I enjoy doing the will of Him who created me. It is my honor to serve and worship before Him with time, talent and deeds.

It is very gratifying to know before the world was formed, I was chosen by Him to be a part of His Kingdom-building and leading other souls to Christ. Even though anyone who is born again will tell you, the road in doing so isn't always easy and definitely not glamorous as the world would describe as fashionable or earthshattering on the outside.

However, concerning the spiritual benefits of being "connected to Him" and being His son or daughter for

Kingdom-building, absolutely nothing else can ever compare to the feeling of being a champion in His army of winners. Being part of God's plan is priceless and more than worth it all in the end.

> *"The only way out of your personal storm is your willingness and courage to tunnel through it to the other side of victory!"*
>
> *Brenda Murphy*

> *"Remember what I told you: 'A servant is not greater than his master. If they persecuted me, they will persecute you also. If they obeyed my teaching, they will obey yours also.'"*
>
> John 15:20 (NIV)

IV. YOU CALL ME LORD—MAY I CALL YOU SERVANT?

September 2012, I arrived home from work on a Thursday evening around 6:15 pm, parked in the garage and came in through the side door of my house. I walked into our office and found my beloved spouse and covering on the floor of our office, curled up in a fetal position. I didn't know what happened or what was wrong.

To say it took the breath out of me would be a gross understatement. I screamed his name and cried out to the Lord, asking Him to help us. The process of calling 9-1-1 and allowing the dispatcher to walk me through aiding my spouse until EMS arrived was extremely overwhelming.

I continued to focus on the name of Jesus as I attended to Audie. When the EMS attendants arrived, they immediately started working on him to keep him stable until he arrived at the hospital. In the meantime, I remember staring at him, thinking to myself, "This has to be a bad nightmare."

The strangest thing happened in that moment. One of the attending EMT personnel was walking out of our front door when he suddenly stopped and turned around. Before he wheeled the gurney out the door with my husband, he asked, "Ma'am, do you mind if I prayed with you for your husband's healing?"

I was touched and quickly said, "Please. I would really appreciate that."

We prayed, and he walked out to join the remaining crew who patiently waited for him to get into the truck. I was hurt but humbled even with all that was going on. God still showed up through the compassion of that gentleman that day to let me know all was going to be well.

After Audie was admitted into the hospital, and the work began to save his life and assist him on his way back to recovery, I never left his side other than for work. The most thought-provoking thing happened to me during this entire ordeal to keep my head up and trusting in God.

I wasn't overwhelmingly frightened, even when they diagnosed a severe and massive stroke. Somehow even in the midst of this very trying time, I felt enormously "comforted," as if a greater power carried me through the process step-by-step. I literally experienced everything from what to say, to when to say it—when to be silent and how to carry out the exact order of business when necessary.

Daily I don't think my spiritual feet ever touched the ground. Constantly, I felt as though I merely observed my body from up above through the lens of a powerful supernatural microscope from afar. No matter from what angle my situation appeared, the lenses I was permitted to look through were always crystal clear and unfiltered.

I was given instructions every day of what to do and who to speak to about what particular concern or issues that had arisen or was in the process of being warranted. Funny now, looking back on it all, sometimes even before a crisis arose or I was notified by staff at the hospital about issues, I was always prepared.

At other times, I would be prompted as to what to say and what not to say, who to call for encouragement and who to turn to for a listening ear and shelter while in the spiritual storm.

I sensed all along the comforting I was exposed to could not have been from anyone else but God who was indeed ordering my personal steps each and every moment. I cannot remember a time when I was unattended to.

One day in the process of our journey, the Spirit of the Lord spoke to my heart and said, "You call me Lord. May I call you servant?"

Wow! I thought.

As I meditated on that Word, I asked God to please interpret that concept for me, because I definitely wanted to understand its meaning.

The thought came to me that as a believer, I never second guessed my relationship with God. I recognized Him daily as being my Savior, Redeemer, Keeper, Deliverer and Provider (to name a few). However, in His presence, I felt like for the first time, I was being asked to identify how I intimately saw our relationship as a whole. And more importantly, how did He view me in His presence during that time?

Realizing I truly depended upon Him for everything— mainly for my sanity and peace of mind. All during the day, I constantly looked to Him for balance, strength in my walk, renewing of my godly character through my response and in my interaction with others, especially when I was under tremendous pressure and dealing with the public at large.

I soon came to a conclusion. While I knew without a shadow of a doubt I could lean on and depend upon God for His faithfulness, it never really crossed my mind whether or not God felt the same way about Himself being able to depend upon me to be readily available and willing to execute His will for my life at a moment's notice—even while being under spiritual construction or attack.

When I replayed the statement in my mind, "You call me Lord. May I call you servant?" It caused me to think about how often I would make myself available to Him when He desired to use me for his divine purpose in my life.

It made me stop and take notice of how I reacted to the call. Would I eagerly go, or did I have to be coerced? Would I have to be paid, or would I go just because I was grateful He alone saw the greater in me and consistently carried me all the way, affording me the means to make His purpose and will known through me?

After spending much needed quiet time alone with my thoughts, I came to the decision that He was asking me if I trust Him enough in my daily personal life to allow Him to really order and reconstruct my steps, no matter where He would lead me and for how long it would take for me to spiritually arrive. Would I be obedient enough to follow wherever the destination might take me?

Loving Him as I do, it was a no-brainer to say yes! Without total access to the full blueprint of it all. Even though I love Him, there were times I was still nervous, apprehensive and scared because the thought of possibly being without Him for even a minute or a second was out of the question and much too difficult to even entertain. Yet, I was still curious at times and willing to go wherever He ordered my steps.

Things were happening so incredibly fast I barely had an opportunity to catch my breath in between crises. Being able to remain sane under various trials caused me to rely upon past experiences and outcomes He had already brought and delivered me through.

Knowing this fueled an unprecedented fire under my feet to continue to forge ahead, trusting in his promises and provisions all the way—even when the outside parameter shouted, "Bleak, bleak, bleak."

I fully understood I could take God at His word because His track record, His history, His Name was always spotless and true. Where He was guiding me now, I had no fear He was definitely more than able and capable of accommodating and keeping me and my spouse.

Along the way, the three of us entered some dark and narrow pathways. Some dangerous, rough and jagged terrains. Some twists and to Audie and me, definitely some unforeseen turns. But no matter the journey's trails, I was always assured I would arrive safely to my assigned destination.

> *"Just because I was willing to follow Him does not mean that sometimes I wasn't afraid, nervous, and apprehensive. At times, I didn't necessarily understand the journey. However, I learned in the process, how to trust, lean and depend upon His personal references: grace, mercy, goodness and faithfulness for my safe arrival."*
>
> Brenda Murphy

Over time, my husband was in the hospital and rehabilitation for a period of three months. I watched the gracious arm of God carefully direct us through rough times, lean times, challenging times and sometimes even very difficult times.

What I learned in those exasperating moments was always to keep my eyes and my faith on the tour guide and never to lose sight of his instructions for my daily walking strategies and victories.

To me the name "Lord" means someone who watches over me and my wellbeing. He is the gatekeeper and lover of my soul. He is the protector of my daily benefits and provisions. He is the Counselor, Shield, the Source and Resource of my very existence. He is the daily Supplier of my Substance in all things.

The more conscious I became of this fact, the more I felt an awareness of the personal shifting in how I looked at our relationship. Scared and all, I knew I had to draw closer to Him for my personal survival. I longed to be nearer to Him. Feeling close to His presence made all the difference in the world to me.

For the first time in my walk with Christ, I, probably like so many others, focused more on my needs and desires when it came to prayer. I did not factor in what God needed from me or the type of commitment it would really take to wholeheartedly follow Him no matter what the cost.

That question of "You call Me Lord. May I call you servant?" resonated in me like none other. It took me months to come to grips with the true concept of it all. At the end of this timeframe, I concluded what He was asking of me was to accept the fact I can totally depend upon Him for every need, desire, problem or situation, whether it appeared to be suddenly or a long time coming.

He wanted to know if I would rely upon Him whether the situation became more intensified or not. I needed to be mindful of His presence being around me and to become more attuned at any given time or place. I needed to understand I for one, would not be in charge of the how and when it was going to take place.

I believe God wanted to know from me whether I was in a crisis, situation or any circumstance, He could still depend on me to carry out the purposes and plans He designed for my life to others in those instances. Even when it was quite obvious, at least in the moment, that I didn't understand in my flesh what was going on from one moment to the next with my life.

He wanted to know if I would be faithful to Him while being mishandled, disheveled, hurdled along from one incomplete resolution to the next, distressed and sometimes discouraged by life's outcomes. He perhaps wanted to know if I would trust Him even at times when from my end, I couldn't trace Him. Or, would I simply pick the battles that were less cumbersome to associate myself with Him while being challenged by life's stormy weather.

It is interesting to think Jesus would actually need those who love Him to be available and willing to work in conjunction with the leading of the Holy Spirit to carry out His will here on earth.

And at the very least when it seemed the most inopportune time and my life was most chaotic, there arose one of the most important questions of my life. There are some people in the world today who may feel as though God could not possibly need the assistance of mankind to carry out His earthly plan, because He is God. And He doesn't need our approval to do anything.

Until my personal experiences, I generally thought God

could and would do whatever He pleased for whomever without the aide and/or assistance of anyone else. He simply spoke, and it came to fruition. And yes, He can, and it would. However, through my experiences, I now have been very much enlightened with the fact God uses His people to work through to transport His blessings to others.

I get it that our God created us to serve Him through our worship and to carry out His purposes throughout the nation until all of mankind knows His name and sees His works through His people. Each born-again believer is the chosen vessel God desires to use at will and through our obedience to Him.

Clearly God does not "need" us per se to "do" anything. We should not have the attitude that if we were unwilling to serve, no assignment would be completed.

However, what I am trying to say is we were created to make a difference and an impact in the lives of others we meet while here on this earth—primarily beginning in our own home structure first, and then spreading it outwardly to other people, cities, and nations.

Being a servant of the Most High has taught me I am not here to simply serve myself and those I care about only. The mission and purposes are far greater and farther reaching than just confined to my neck of the woods.

I am to seek God about His daily plan and purpose for my life and my life's mission. I am to serve Him and strive to live my life to execute His purpose in what I was created to do by serving others as He leads me to.

"Whoever wants to be great must become a servant."

Mark 10:43 (MSG)

The Message Bible says it well. *"Whoever wants to be "great" must become a servant."* There is absolutely no other way. After all, my sole purpose on earth should be to do the will of God in whatever capacity I am called to. In my humble opinion, no job is too small or too large, especially if it pleases my Lord and Savior.

I know all too well for most people the word "servant" alone sends cold chills down their spines, let alone the thought of serving others whom they may deem are socially and economically beneath their status. I personally have met others who felt that type of servanthood is beneath their logic or comprehension. Therefore, they would rather live perhaps in exile rather than conform to that type of mindset.

Admittedly, I must confess I don't fully understand that mindset. Jesus served from day one on earth and left us example after example in which to follow Him. Yet we still choose to turn a deaf ear and blind eye to that concept.

Because increasingly there is more and more of a need to be served rather than serving; the average person doesn't even give it a thought to being acknowledged as a servant. They would rather be known by bigger "titles and for their entitlements."

At best, if the need arises, they may "help" a little here and there, but in the grand scheme of things, sometimes the attitude is, "Don't expect me to be there every time, because I have my own life and problems to attend to."

I remember approaching a gentleman in a store I managed. Truly he was more than financially equipped to make a donation to a ministry cause, especially since he commanded and demanded everything done for him was "superb," completed to his specifications and perfection.

Heads would roll if they weren't. He would have no problem letting everyone know the mess-up came from you if you didn't jump the moment he said so.

Anyway, one morning he came in a little bit early from his normal routine, and we began chatting as we occasionally did. I asked him if he would consider making a small donation to this particular ministry. I will never forget the cold, smirking, heartless remark he made that day.

He said, "Brenda, be assured that we, meaning he and his wife, only make donations to charities and associations we consider as meaningful." Believe it or not, I realize it was after all their money, and they could indeed do with it whatever they wanted to. However, to add a sharp, demeaning undertone was unnecessary and just mean-spirited. That "extra" was done so I would catch his drift of how he felt in particular. I looked him in his eyes fighting the tears back and simply said, "Noted." I never asked again.

One thing is crystal clear to me personally. When I have a misguided understanding of something, I will automatically fight against it, because I don't have a clear cut revelation of what is being required or asked of me. Therefore, I am uncomfortable with exactly how I am to respond or react to the request. This taught me that rather than come up with my own philosophy about it, I must seek God immediately for understanding instead.

While servanthood clearly means to serve others, it does not or should not mean we should revert to becoming a doormat or a slave at the beck and call of someone else's request to do "everything" just because they ask.

Being a servant of God's goal for my life is to seek His will for my life over everything and everyone else's opinions, thoughts, ideas and even their opinionated suggestions. I should not assume that just because I am talented or gifted to operate in a specific gifting, I should allow it to be used at the beck and call of others for their pleasure or enjoyment. Instead I am to seek God, inquiring whether it is actually something pleasing to my Master.

I am learning above all things and in all situations and circumstances, my first stop should be at the Master's feet for wisdom, peace, insight, grace and power to get the task at hand done in His timing, will, and for His purpose.

If the idea, project, task or position is being filled by me, for me, and not the will of the Almighty God, it is classified as a failure before I even start. Lesson learned for myself is never; ever take a role or a position from someone or something that is unwilling, unable or incapable of sustaining you in the process of the assignment being asked of you.

In order to stay on point with my purpose, it is my desire now more than ever to make a conscious effort daily to seek the plan for the day from God before I get out of bed. This goal has now become the priority of my obedience to the will of God and my personal growth in Kingdom building.

I realize the struggle to accomplish the task assigned by God becomes more and more weakened when the details of the plan are being followed for my life by God. In other words, He will provide every aspect of the needs necessary for me to accomplish the journey.

The phrase, "Can I call you servant?" lets me know God is quite concerned about details and specifics in the plans He has for my life. Sure I can simply go out daily and do a bunch of things I think are "good" or godly. But they may not be necessarily what He would qualify as "Kingdom building or pleasing in His sight." Among the many attributes of God, I am becoming more and more aware that He is indeed a strategist over my life.

A strategist is a person with responsibility for the formulation and implementation of a strategy. Strategy generally involves setting goals, determining actions to reach and achieve the goals, and mobilizing resources to execute the actions.

> *"See, I have set before thee this day life and good, and death and evil; In that I command thee this day to love the LORD thy God, to walk in his ways, and to keep his commandments and his statutes and his judgments, that thou mayest live and multiply: and the LORD thy God shall bless thee in the land whither thou goest to possess it. But if thine heart turn away, so that thou wilt not hear, but shalt be drawn away, and worship other gods, and serve them;"*
>
> Deuteronomy 30:15-20 KJV

The first thing I must do is choose whose plans and way I am going to follow for my life. If I choose God to lead, guide and direct me in my daily goings, I must also be willing to adhere to His ways and directions for my life.

He alone is the only All-Knowing God who fully understands my uprising and my sitting down, the head count of every strand of hair on my head and the direction in which my life will take. Even still, I am charged to make a decision I am willing to be governed by for my life.

To do it any other way is like going out of my way shopping to buy a gift for someone without taking into consideration their likes or dislikes at all. Instead, I choose to purchase the gift with only myself in mind as opposed to what I know they would enjoy or really need and hope somehow magically they like it as well. That's not thinking of them at all. That is just me being selfish.

I also have to factor in the things I choose to do that require little to no effort or relinquishing of my control still may not be the things God is requiring of me the most.

For example, waving at my neighbor from across the street as I am entering into my driveway is simple. It requires little to no effort or sacrifice on my part. However; hearing God say make dinner tonight and take it to that neighbor's house, or take them out to dinner instead. My following up on that request and denying my flesh in the process of participating in what I know I heard the Holy Spirit saying is a whole different animal.

There is nothing worse for me than for someone to say with great excitement, "Brenda, I brought something special for you. Something I just know you have always wanted." How disappointing to find out not only did I not want it, but it was not even my type, color, desire or need. It was something the person perhaps wanted to get rid of, had too many of or simply gave it to me without any thought, purpose, or with me in mind.

> *"So why do you keep calling me 'Lord, Lord!' when you don't do what I say?"*
>
> Luke 6:46-47

No one likes to be ignored or disrespected, especially God. I ask myself why I would cry out to Him for help or turn to Him for direction for my life. Then as He directs me, I say to Him, "No that's not right, or, that doesn't make sense." As I go my own way only to be disappointed, disillusioned and dejected, why am I surprised when things do not turn out my way or go horribly wrong?

In most cases when this type of approach happens to us, we sometimes have a tendency to blame God even though we deliberately ignored His plans for our lives at the outset and went our own way. There will be times when we honestly do not use better judgment in our response or approach to God and how He specifically set the plan for our day.

Sometimes, we have a tendency to think we know a better way and insight to accomplish the task He has set before us. We do not realize the importance of never deviating away from detailed plans God has for our lives. And when we do, it could end up being not only a bad decision, but not favorable in the outcome for us as well.

> "Servanthood is about having the willingness and the humbleness to serve out of our obedience to God even before we witness the outcome of the purpose."
>
> Brenda Murphy

Knowing I serve a tremendous, all knowing, all seeing, capable, unlimited God somehow puts all of my dysfunctionalities to rest and provides a sense of incredible ease when I find myself getting a little out-of-shape and start to go my own way. I quickly say to myself, "Wait. Are you sure you want to go this alone without the aide and assistance of the Holy Spirit?"

I am grateful I have grown enough to notice the

difference in my overall desire of trusting in my own manmade abilities, mindset and strength as opposed to seeking the wisdom, guidance and dependency from my Creator first. I certainly have experienced enough heartache in the midst of it all to know for sure it is no longer my preference to attempt to go it alone when I do not ever have to — especially since risk-taking is no longer my forte.

Like others, it took a whole lot of bumps in the worldly road for me to understand my opinions, thoughts, ideas and plans are no earthly match for my Heavenly Father's wisdom, guidance and protection. Jesus isn't just familiar with me. He isn't just acquainted with me, and He hasn't just met me. He is my Redeemer, my Creator, my Lord and my personal Savior. He alone has set the foundation for my life in place, and my daily steps are ordered by Him.

"When thou passest through the waters, I will be with thee; and through the rivers, they shall not overflow thee: when thou walkest through the fire, thou shalt not be burned; neither shall the flame kindle upon thee."

Isaiah 43:2 (KJV)

V. MY GREATEST STRENGTH WAS PROVEN IN MY SMALLEST TEST

After finding a lump in my right breast in March 2014, the subsequent surgery in May 2014 and receiving radiation treatment in June 2014, life for me began a series of various siftings, each for my spiritual and earthly good. But they took a very drastic change on my physical man.

The shift required more of me thinking and reacting on a grander plain. I no longer could operate and/or function on the level I currently resided. I knew instantly, if for no other real reason, my livelihood and that of my spouse and I required a deeper, definite and precocious thought process as it related to our survival in God.

We could no longer wait on God bringing us the answers we desperately needed. I came to the conclusion after reading and re-reading the Word of God, He alone had already pre-deposited the answers to our situation within each of us.

In fact, the greater the trial, the more assured and intensely I felt the answers were near us. In fact they would reside within our spoken word of our faith and our belief.

Day by day, we chose to cling to the only real source we knew. The Source that by now had become our only Resource, Provision and Stability.

As we continued to rely upon the Name of Jesus, we encountered various examples of His wondrous works and His random kindness towards us. What I mean by random works is that you could not necessarily put your finger on how He was going to move in our lives each day.

Our job in trusting God was like this: Get up in the morning, praying and thanking Him. Get dressed and bless His Name for strength and hope. Praise Him for unseen provision and every tiny conceivable need we didn't even know we needed being met and being surpassed beyond any stretch of our own physical comprehension.

In fact, the wisdom, knowledge and breakthroughs God gave me is not to be compared with anything I have ever walked through, walked out of or that came against me. The gracious hand of God definitely hoovered over and on occasions, rested, ruled and abided over me continuously. At moments, I felt endowed in His presence. Encompassed by His care for me and my household.

Honestly, for the most part, my normal routine as I was accustomed to living never returned back to what most perhaps would identify as "normal." I knew personally, it never would again. Suddenly it seemed as though all I previously thought I knew no longer mattered nor applied.

Even as I look at myself today in the mirror, I recognized the woman I am looking at from the outside. But I know without a shadow of a doubt, the woman I used to be on the inside has moved on to greater heights and an even greater love and respect for the purpose for which she was birthed into this earth and destined to become.

This woman is more concreted and assured in the Lord

and her relationship with Him today. Her willingness to be dependent and reliant upon Him is more gracious now than ever before.

She recognizes that having Christ as the center of her joy and learning to relinquish herself day by day is teaching her and growing her in supernatural ways of how to become more sober minded while sojourning through life's upheavals and mishaps. She's learning only God can bring the right people at the right time into her life when she needs them most.

She knows what it means to rest in the arms of an Almighty, relentless Savior. He is quicker than quick and more than able to do exceedingly and abundantly more than she can either think or imagine possible for her life.

She knows there is no safer place to be than in the expressed will, purpose and arms of the ALMIGHTY God. And she is learning how to bask in each and every moment of their time spent together. She has a newfound love, respect and gratitude for this woman. She encourages her daily and champions her to keep it moving.

She knows she is deeply loved by God. Approved of Him, cherished and watched over by Him. She gets it that He first loved her, and He will always see her through no matter what. She knows He will never undermine her, be embarrassed by her or cast her aside.

She doesn't have to work to try to earn His love, validation, or approval. She fully knows and appreciates her best days are directly ahead of her, while His greatness rests in her. Just knowing that sets her free from all earthly condemnation freely expressed by mankind.

Because of those new revelations, I now recognize through the love and strength of Jesus, I am much more resilient, resourceful, patient, compassionate and thankful for every waking moment of my life. I value each and every precious minute of it spent with the people I love and cherish daily.

I take absolutely nothing and no one near and dear to me for granted. I make it a point to keep in contact by any means necessary to hear their voice, laugh with them, celebrate with them and even cry with them if the time spent together is warranted and beneficial.

Daily I find myself thanking God for every deliberate and intentional life lesson learned in my journey. I value and appreciate what He is trying to teach me at every venture. I am more focused in my stride of life, and I try to live my life in the moment around me and not allow myself to get caught up in unnecessary pomp and circumstance.

I am learning not to sweat the little unimportant things that have no credibility or add any significant value to my days. I choose to ignore those nuisances that use to drain me mentally dry and physically despondent, offering nothing in return.

After entering into this journey, the first genuine thing I understood I had to do was to surrender my complete will, thoughts, fears and all my doubts over to God. This was a challenge to my flesh in the very beginning. Because I was one that needed to see where I was being lead first. Further into the journey, now I was learning there was just no room at all in my flesh to try to figure out what to do next.

It was my expressed intent not to involve others, whether directly connected to me by blood or mere acquaintance, to advise me on what steps to take next. I understood for sure the only two people involved in this fight was me and Jesus.

And I was learning that whereas Psalm 37:23 says, the *"Steps of a good man were ordered by the Lord; and that He, delighteth in His way."* It was vital I understood the ordering of first steps came from God. For my steps to be ordered, I must first learn and accept the discipline and maturity it requires to take ownership of that particular step.

There is a maturity and a level of respons-i-bility that goes along with each step ordered by the Lord. God wants to know that once we have accepted our role in taking ownership of where that step leads us in carrying out His will for our lives, we can then take personal respons-ibility for our actions and role in that assignment.

In other words, we cannot pass our accountabilities on to the shoulders or the hands of another. If we want a house and have been praying and asking God for that property, once God opens that door for us to become a homeowner, we cannot and should not expect someone else to make sure the house upkeep is being done by someone else. The responsibility does not belong to anyone but me.

I cannot demand for others to respect me as a "grown adult" when the moment or the mood fits me. But when the pressure and stressors of life happen to me, then I run back to the changing room and put on all of my baby clothes and wail like an infant incapable of taking on the responsibility.

> *The steps of a good man are ordered by the LORD:*
> *and he delighteth in his way.*
>
> Psalm 37:23 (KJV)

So in order for me to stay afloat, I had to become more and more God-centered and reliant upon His name to keep me on the right path. I could not allow any unnecessary distractions or detractions to take over and lead me astray.

I knew it would be in Him and through Him I would be able to live, move and have my expressed being. I knew by inviting others into my journey at that particular moment would be asking a baby to fly a Boeing 747 for the first time without a pilot license or any forward training. That baby would be untrained and ill-equipped to pilot the plane successfully. And not only that, but you expect an inevitable crash soon thereafter.

In my quest to draw closer to the Lord, I wasn't just seeking victory. I desired to be on the other side of victory with room to spare. I didn't just want to be out of the frying pan. I didn't even want to be near the kitchen period.

If I were to survive this trek, it was going to take something and someone much greater, wiser, dependable and all-knowing to bring me out—not just barely but as more than a conqueror. So I "learned" how to cast my "everything" upon God about my personal journey, fears, doubts and my phobias.

I had to surrender my flesh to the will of God so I could "trust" Him completely. No one else could do it for me. No one else but God could possibly understand what it took to hold on to my sanity or reasoning in those moments of being truly stretched and challenged to indescribable measures.

During those defying moments, my flesh wanted to betray me through my thoughts of negativity fighting against me for every promise I knew God had promised me through His Word, like *"No weapon formed against you shall prosper, and every tongue which rises against you in judgment You shall condemn. This is the heritage of the servants of the LORD, and their righteousness is of Me."* Isaiah 54:17b (KJV) Or, *"Behold, I will bring it health and cure, and I will cure them, and will reveal unto them the abundance of peace and truth."* Jeremiah 33:6 (KJV)

In my most perplexing hours, I found His perfect peace surpassed my understanding daily, because I made a conscious effort to seek His face whether it was through reading, meditation, praying or listening to praise and worship music.

I understood the only way I could continually experience and receive His peace was for me to deliberately seek His presence in and over my life. In other words, because I was seeking Him, He was looking for me. Ready, willing, capable and able.

In fact, the more I rested in Him, I knew I could trust His name and His provision in every step and move I made. He talked with me about decisions I needed to make. And I adhered to His plans for my life. Each time I did so, I experienced victory!

Daily through trusting God, He aligned my schedule so my path would cross others that would prove to be a tremendous blessing in my life. Through those He spiritually appointed for my journey, it was no surprise to me when they "just" showed up on time and in time to make my task for that day easy.

There is a gospel song written by Reverend James Moore that says, "He was there all the time, He was there all the time; Waiting patiently in line, He was there all the time." I am a living, viable witness. He was indeed there "ALL" of the time. There is no mistaking His awesome presence in every crevice of my life and my eternal soul. There is no one greater than our God!

I knew when He showed up there would be a resounding, undeniable powerful presence that would leave an undeniable footprint proving He indeed was the One that carried me through to the other side of my journey safely. Sometimes it seemed I was ahead of schedule.

When He showed up in the presence of my test, He commanded the attention of all who played a viable role in my healing. He was there, and He was overwhelmingly capable to handle whatever life threw at me and more, because He wasn't just on the sidelines watching from afar, He had crossed over ahead of me and "made" all of my crooked paths plain!

> *"I learned when I took the time to make God first in my life, He made sure I was never last."*
>
> Brenda Murphy

From day one, the doctors were astonished. The radiologists were amazed, and the nurses just simply joined me in my daily praise and adoration of His holy name. In other words, no one was shy about giving God glory at all, and I totally loved every moment of it.

The staff recognized His presence in the room, and they got in on the excitement with each accomplishment. Each day of treatment was met with praise, so God automatically received ALL of the glory.

The first time, I was scheduled for radiation for 15 minutes. I was nervous about allowing the chemicals to enter into my body. However, while I was being prepped for the process, I began to allow my mind to think about what Christ had already done for me over the years and even that very day.

As I commenced resting in Him, I felt His amazing peace, which felt like liquid rain showering over my natural body into my spiritual mindset. It brought me instant assurance Daddy was present in the room with me, protecting and guarding those things that mattered most to me and my family.

Not even five minutes into the actual treatment, I felt an enormous weight lifting off of me, and His peace ensued seemingly every cell in my body. His peace excelled the intensity of the actual radiation being administered into my body.

In fact, it was at that exact moment I knew. While the radiation was being administered, God's power was ministering directly into my soul and signifying to me all I needed to do was simply surrender my will for His.

It felt incredible to be held in the arms of the Lord, knowing for sure His presence was surrounding me before, during and after the treatment. As I closed my eyes into absolute surrender, I heard a soft, gentle whisper say, "Remember, before the radiation ever penetrates your body, my blood has already covered you over 2,000 years ago. No fear."

The only thing that kept me on that table was dignity! Spiritually, I had personally vacated the premises and was giving God a standing ovation for the marvelous work He had already done in my body, as if I had already completed my entire treatment plan.

The nurse advocates asked if I wanted to listen to any particular music during this process, and I said, "Yes, but nothing sad or somber. In fact, please raise the volume up a notch so we can really praise Him. How about something like "How Great Is Our God?" I asked.

The nurse smiled and said, "We can do that."

And the three of us jammed for the next 15 minutes.

Needless to say, during the year 2014, I learned so much about God's grace, mercy and His provision for my life and my family. I treasured coming into the knowledge of what

His grace and mercies were all about, and how they were gifts that kept on reproducing themselves over and over again in my life.

I was learning how grace was such a gentleman and respective of my personal need for Him in my life and daily routine. Equally so, grace eagerly awaited to escort me into various aspects of my day, making sure I sought the wisdom and direction of God for that day.

> "Mercy is the kindness, necessity, absolute sheer favor of God's goodness when He doesn't even have to be powerful, influencing our daily existence upon the earth. This is not something we can ever earn or deserve to partake of. It's just His goodness and at will service He provides on a daily basis."
>
> Brenda Murphy

For most people, generally speaking, grace and mercy are not even a relevant thought or viable notion that this great gift is ever present in their daily lives. It is oftentimes overlooked and grossly underappreciated.

Sometimes it does not appear important in the grand scheme of their everyday lifestyle. It is taken for granted tomorrow will come or the days and years following will magically happen.

Some never once stop to think about what if it were possible for God to withdraw His incredible grace and mercy from them. Where then would they be or where would they go?

It's amazing to me. When an unsurmountable problem that is not easily fixed or changed in the twinkling of an eye or through man's own limited strength and might, all of sudden, the search is on to "find God" for immediate answers and explanations and yes, even miracles.

There is something about trouble, problems, issues and circumstances that always drive us to God and the need to be in His presence in that moment. It doesn't matter whether it is through fear, doubt, uncertainty or an absence of some sort for most, God is our go-to person.

It is in those specific times, when our backs are against the wall and when we finally come to the end of ourselves, we realize there must be someone higher than ourselves. We must seek and call upon Him for help and true deliverance. Nothing else will do.

So it is with testing. Testing has a way of showing up with little or sometimes no direct warning, and it doesn't always give notice when it may leave or what the outcome of the testing will be in its aftermath. Testing for me in the natural can show up as a form of process of elimination.

It really has no control over me. But if I am caught off guard and am not aware of what the Word of God has said about my test in the manner in which I should view it, that test can, and often times does, wreak havoc like nobody's business in my life.

When testing finds me unsure about my faith, belief, wisdom and even my trust in God, in the process, it often renders me disturbed with self-doubt and self-inflicted overwhelmedness and unsure about everything. Testing brings with it what I called unimaginable side-effects that can be incurable if left unattended.

Side-effects like long-term stress often lead to other long-term medical issues. The need to worry about how things will eventually turn out ahead of time can lead to disorders that cause other medical issues.

Life's tests also carry with them the feeling of helplessness, hopelessness and defeat. When all of these conflicts move in for the kill, at times in my past, I have questioned everything that happens in that moment.

I learned while I was being tested, if I found myself unfamiliar with what the Word or the promise of God said about that particular situation, I was not confident about how to stand in that certain moment.

Because of my lack of knowledge about that particular promise, I allowed my emotions to dictate my response and inform me I was defeated. I became considerably overwhelmed, even to the place where I thought for a moment the storm could just overtake me.

I began to notice a great truth. When I was able to lay hold of Scripture and read the promises of God for myself out loud while in that particular situation and chose to believe that spoken promise for my own life, I felt it was enough fuel for me to continue moving forward in confidence.

More than ever, I knew for sure my daily walk had to "become" more than just going through a morning routine of memorizing various scripture references, recanting Bible stories without fully standing in faith and believing God was Almighty and cannot fail in all of His promises to me. I had to simply believe the Word of God for my life and apply muscle to my faith while doing so.

When I took the Word of God to heart for myself and chose to stand firm that He was able to do exceedingly and abundantly above and even beyond what I could think or even imagine, I was always victorious in my endeavors, even when I had to tunnel through the trial. I knew God was always at the helm looking out for me.

One of the important things I learned the most about testing is it does not always challenge me in my private moments when no one else is around or aware.

Though testing has no respecter of persons, zip codes, pedigree, age limits social status or boundaries; it doesn't care about our financial security, wealth, success rate or educational background. Times of trials and testing come to all at one time or the other.

Testing and trials don't knock. They don't ask for permission to enter into our lives. None of them ask if this is a convenient time or venue for you to meet. They don't care if you are in a good place in your life or overall well-being. Trials and testing just come, and sometimes when one of them show up, it is known to stay for a while — convenient or not.

Testing will interrupt your flow at a moment's notice. It can crumble even the strongest marriage if allowed. It often shreds livelihoods, demolishes families, wreaks havoc in your health, cancels careers, shatters ministries, and devastates dreams and desires — especially during those times when you may think you have it all together.

Testing comes to rattle the cage and to shake the very foundation on which we build our lives and our legacies. When it moves on to others, sometimes it can leave us overwhelmed, bewildered and baffled if we are ill-prepared and unfamiliar with its intent.

It can also leave us extremely bitter and very judgmental of others' progress as well, even though we are clueless as to what they may be going through or coming out of.

I have personally witnessed testing interrupting the

most solid family structure and bringing the well-versed individuals to their spiritual or natural knees with little advance notice about its reasoning for doing so.

Because there is a natural tendency to flight in the face of fear and doubt on the other end of the spectrum, often our choice, sad to say, is not always to turn to Jesus first. Many times when His name is called out, our thoughts and dependency upon His ability to bring us out and through can be far removed from the matter at hand.

As nerve-racking as fear can be, I learned there is an amazing flip side to it. One is not always addressed and is sometimes very easily overlooked. According to Joyce Meyer, while the acronym for fear is F.E.A.R. (False Evidence Appearing Real), I found there's no true threat of immediate physical danger in the wake of fear itself.

Remember the word "appearing" means it hasn't happened yet but could quite possibly do so in the near future. F.E.A.R. is an illusion to unlimited imaginary possibilities the mind can formulate well on its own capabilities.

Fear is something we fabricate in our own minds and assume is real according to www.copyblogger.com/f-e-a-r/, especially when we dwell on the negative too long, giving it a foothold in our thinking.

I love Pastor Creflo Dollar's version better. "Fear tolerated is Faith Contaminated." Well said. If allowed, fear will not only shut down every positive promise God has spoken over my life, it will also turn the lights out on every dream, hope, peace, possibility or chance I have ever imagined for my life. Fear will dog me until I relentlessly just totally surrender and admit, even if under direct pressure, I am not good enough for the job, the promotion, the marriage or the relationship if I allow it to.

Until I realized my greatest potential and needs can be resolved only through the blood of Jesus and His unconditional love for me, I was allowing the enemy to prevail over me each and every time. And I was left with only regrets, dismay and sometimes even heartache.

I knew if I was to see the salvation of God, and be delivered from self-inflicted doubts and unbelief, I had to change and challenge my personal perspective over virtually everything in my life.

If I remotely stood a chance at victory in any particular area in my life, I needed to make up my mind to know exactly what God's Word said about me, to me and for me. I needed to seriously think about what I was thinking about and change my spiritual focus.

> *"For in him we live, and move, and have our being; as certain also of your own poets have said, For we are also his offspring."*
>
> Acts 17:28 (KJV)

Seeing the "salvation of the Lord" to me is not just about being spiritually saved from going to hell. It's more about being delivered, soundness of mind, healing in my soul and building up my inner man.

Being able to fully embrace "salvation" affords me the opportunity to escape from everything that once held me captive and kept me from seeing the wonderful loving person I was created to be in the image of God to begin with.

True salvation is embracing the freedom and liberty to live at peace first of all with myself. Then to embrace wholeheartedly my journey through my faults, failures and flaws, and to still know I am created for the Master's use.

Not after I clean myself up or get the big promotion or marry the right guy—no. I can receive salvation today and become anew in Jesus right now!

Monday, July 27, 2015 my life changed for the better in an awe inspiring kind of way. Over that particular weekend, I had a painful incident happen to me concerning my teeth. Realizing pretty much all dentist offices were closed over the weekend, I attended to my mouth as best I could and quietly prayed God would have the answer for me on Monday as to where I should go for treatment.

After arriving to work on Monday morning, needless to say, I was still very much perplexed over the weekend situation, and I decided to take a break and once again consult God about my steps being ordered as it related to finding the "right dentist." In doing so, before I could finish putting in my request, the Holy Spirit had provided me with a name to contact regarding the issue.

Not wasting any time at all, I immediately grabbed my phone and made contact with the dentist office revealed. Considering the fact, I had not spoken nor had any contact with this doctor in probably over 8-10 years, his receptionist was very professional and placed me on hold to inquire about my need for a dentist that day.

Little did I know, when she returned back to the phone she replied, "Brenda can you come in today around 12:00 pm?"

Shocked, but extremely excited I said, "Yes, I absolutely can."

After arriving at the dentist office and spending a brief moment in his chair, I was met with what appeared to me with very devastating news regarding my teeth.

I literally started to cry as I thought about just how trying my life and medical history had been over the past five years. While in the middle of receiving this news, I quietly heard the Holy Spirit say to me, "Brenda, share your story with him. Open your mouth and say something." And so I did. As I called the doctor's name, I felt the strength of my Heavenly Father wash over me like liquid love confirming within me, "I got you covered."

I said to the doctor through my tear-stained face, "I don't know how God is going to bring me through this moment, but I just believe He will."

As I shared my story from the beginning to end regarding my spouse and my medical challenges for the past three years, I noticed the doctor's entire countenance change right before my very eyes. Even as the words came out of my mouth, I was frightened to hear just how much danger, trouble, challenges and situations the Lord had carried me through up to this point.

Even through all the rough patches and unexplained situations, I still had a strong sense God's presence was resting on my behalf. The more I talked, the more I was assured of God's affirmation that He loved me and was going to see me through this very difficult and challenging moment.

I told the doctor about my weekend incident with my teeth and how I made it through the weekend asking God to lead me in the right direction of where to go. I told him during my prayer time with the Lord, his name resonated in my spirit to reach out to for help. I simply felt this was the person/place for me to speak go to visit for my teeth.

I just kept saying it was never my intention to allow my mouth to get in such condition. However, my spouse's health challenges came first, and when he was improving, I would then seek help for myself. I told the doctor I didn't know how God was going to bless me, but I believed He was going to bring me out being more than a conqueror. For me, it was a "God thing."

In that same moment, there was my deliverance along with my answer. God had indeed turned things around in my favor.

The doctor said, "Brenda," and he paused to clear his throat. He composed himself before continuing. "Can you meet me back here in my office at 3:30 pm?"

I could tell in my soul a spiritual shift had changed in the atmosphere and something transpired between him and God as well.

He was adamant about me meeting him back in his office at 3:30 pm that day. It wasn't so much what he said as it was the look in his eyes when he said it. In that moment, I could sense the very presence of God in that room and even through his reaction; I knew it was an indeed a "God thing."

When he finally spoke again, he said, "You know it's a God thing don't you?"

Crying again, I said "Yes, I know."

I could sense perhaps he was a little surprised by his own response to me and his reactions to what perhaps the Holy Spirit was saying to him concerning helping me. Nevertheless, he moved ahead with his decision to help me.

Once I returned back to his office, I received nothing but outstanding and superb customer service all the way. For me that day, I knew I received God's divine purpose and provision, and God's presence allowed the doctor and my paths to cross in my favor.

I was treated with professionalism, perfection and poise from the beginning to the end. The doctor and his entire staff showed me godliness, compassion, integrity and Christ each time an appointment was made. At every appointment when the treatments were over, the doctor would instruct his staff, no charges today. They looked shocked to say the least.

The doctor continued to coach me, encourage me and along the way, he took exceptional care of me and motivated me to continue to move forward with the progress of my teeth. I felt more to them than just a "patient" but more like family in the world of dentistry. They were kind, generous, careful and timely each step of the way.

I will always be grateful and humbled by the favor, genuineness, care and the provision God provided through this very well-known and highly respected doctor. For him to take the time out of his busy schedule to see me, treat me and show kindness to me, I was humbled by it all.

I noticed the hand of God right off through allowing the doctor and his staff to spend time encouraging me in words of wisdom, assuring me things were going to get better, and for taking a personal interest in my mouth. They also gave me top of the line treatment needed for my mouth to remain healthy. I thank him and his team for their overall investment of my health and well-being. Their kindness expressed toward me was simply priceless.

This page intentionally left blank for notes and thoughts.

SECTION TWO

"But seek first His kingdom and His righteousness, and all these things will be added to you." So do not worry about tomorrow; for tomorrow will care for itself. Each day has enough trouble of its own."

Matthew 6:33-34

VI. IT AIN'T WHAT IT LOOKS LIKE

Almost nothing is as it seems. Life's funny that way. Two different people can see an object or a thing in a far distance. Each will declare by their own perception it is one thing while the other individual will declare it is another. However; upon closer observation, it could be neither or something totally different than what they each imagined. So it is with how we perceive each other's life from a distance.

Only God knows the inside of a person's heart, and only He can make that determination as to what is good and what is evil so to speak. In learning to live my life purposefully, I noticed when talking to others I am always questioned about how I could endure so many trials at once. Did I ever think about just throwing in the towel and perhaps simply walking away?

In some ways, I can almost hear in their voices they were just about ready to throw me up under one of the biggest pity parties in the world. They couldn't image any human being walking through what they might deem to be a travesty at best.

I could only imagined what my life must have looked like from outside the parameter of God's divine scope and order for my life. I could sense most, if not all, may have thought, "This is it for her and her husband. There is just absolutely no way they can bounce back from these tragedies."

And for me, that's the best part. That's when I get to share with them God's truth regarding our journey on total healing by God. I didn't bounce back. It was God alone who delivered me through them all and kept me in the midst of it all.

At this stage in my life, I have absolutely no one in the world to impress. Not because I am not special to the Kingdom or no one really cares about me, but because many people do. Because I understand I am running my own race to please no one but the Master and to complete the assignment that has been given my hands to do, I can attest and maybe agree, the testing was quite difficult.

But God stayed His constant vigil over our lives.

When I share my testimony, the most typical response I receive is "Oh my God!" How did you make it through? You've been through so much, you poor thing. God had to have been on your side."

You may ask, "Did you ever feel like just throwing in the towel?"

I thought to myself, "You know what? Believe it or not, the thought never crossed my mind that we were not going to make it. The hard part was learning how to rest and allow the process to serve its purpose through me."

> "It was important to me to understand that all trials and tribulations have an expiration date on them. It's not a matter of when they are coming, just be prepared to rest for the victory when they show up!"
>
> Brenda Murphy

Now if the question was ever asked of me, "Did you ever get tired?"

Absolutely. Did I need a break from it all? Yes, without a doubt. Any real human being would have. Nothing strange or unreasonable about that.

Rather than spending a lot of wasted energy on being bitter, angry, upset, depressed or downtrodden, I recognized these specific tests were sent into our lives to destroy and ridicule us. But God never allows any storm to gain entry into the life of His children without a way of escape. I chose to believe the promises God placed over my life and the life of my family.

I acknowledged these tests were sent in our lives to kill, steal and to destroy us and perhaps even break us and cause us to possibly retreat back from God. But the power of belief in the God I know my family and I serve was greater even in a domino effect of trials. If I could only keep my head up, the King of Glory would in fact come in like a spiritual tidal wave.

When I first noticed the different variations of the testing, I first thought, "Okay, this is a series of testing to see whether or not I am willing to walk it out in faith or give in and wallow in self-defeat."

While I do not know every promise in the Bible, I am told there are more than over 5,300, God has promised. I am quite familiar with a few, and one of the first ones I thought of came from Isaiah 26:3 *"You will keep him in perfect peace, whose mind is stayed on You, Because he trusts in You."* (NKJV)

I learned trusting in God at all times and in all things was so vital. It was extremely important when I was being challenged and tested seemingly from every direction. What I meditated on daily and what I thought about my situation made all the difference in the world—especially when my faith was questioned by others in the wake of a very private family situation.

One of the first things I did was choose to pay close attention to what was coming out of my mouth in conversations. When I did speak, I was very careful to make sure my energy was not wasted, and my time was not spent in vain with individuals who never had my better interest at heart. I could tell just by the first few words into the conversation if they had doubts.

In fact, while many talked and inquired about what directions I was going to take, I was whispering to the Holy Spirit to allow me to please hear what was really being said or asked of me behind the smile or the frown. That way my words lined up with the promises of God and not with the lie of the enemy.

When my strength was being weakened, the very last thing I should do is let my guard down and try to avenge myself through the eyes and limited understanding of others regarding my situation.

No one, other than the pertinent people who really needed to know specific things regarding my spouse's medical challenges, should have details. Those who needed it already had access to his information.

It was not important nor vital for me to engage others in dialogue about things that needed not be answered today or tomorrow. Instead, I simply choose to wait upon God for direction to move forward in the best possible attitude I could.

There were some that would say to me, "Sister Brenda, didn't your husband have a stroke before?"

My reply would be, "Um-hum, yes he did."

I added no more to the conversation at all. I knew God loved me, and He was always pro me from the very beginning. He would undoubtedly bring us through yet another small, irrelevant trial again.

Once I understood God would always be there for me and my family, I choose to believe no matter what state we might find ourselves in, I was definitely going to stay in peace—even if that meant not saying a word.

The enemy absolutely loves to catch us with our defenses down and our attitude anything less than positive. That way, he can get all the glory because of our tiredness and unawareness that he is behind the negativity of it all.

The enemy of this world wanted nothing more than for me to lose it, to doubt God, or to become bitter and angry at the world and everyone in it. He wanted me to think it was our fault were under such trials and testing. I didn't believe the lie and decided to stand still and finish strong, choosing not to wait until the battle was over, but to praise the Lord in my now.

What others may have seen in our situation as a dire trial or circumstance, I saw as two people trusting, leaning, depending and resting in God. Now, let me clarify something here. When I say resting I don't want to give anyone the impression we just laid around the house every day just waiting—doing absolutely nothing but sitting down waiting on God.

Waiting on God means being active in the things you can do through the wisdom and strength God provides to accomplish the task He has set before you for that moment. Resting is not a form of idleness or complacency, but rather a state of alertness in anticipation of how the union between His might and your ability to hear and obey Him will collide, bringing forth the victory you expected in the end.

Admittedly, I did not have any or all of the answers going into the trial. But I can confess I already knew and believed that while travailing through it and while being directly in the midst of it, I had a gut feeling all was indeed well and my very best was just around the corner.

I knew with God's track record and my belief, His word was enough for me. As the days passed and the testing began to loosen its grip on me and my family, I whispered a prayer and silently said, "Thank you, Lord. I can sense this storm is passing over, and I thank You that your gracious arm is resting upon me and my family."

During the storm it is necessary to remain focused and prayed up. It is vital to remain under the shadow of the Almighty God at all times. It is of the utmost urgency to decide to keep your mind on things that are pure, godly and faith-building. Not to do so is just like signing yourself up for hell's boot camp one-on-one.

God wants us to know that even though He didn't bring the storm or cause the storm to form, He is a reliable meteorologist during the storm. You may recall the story in Mark 4:35-41 when Jesus and the disciples were on a particular boat preparing for a journey and a storm was in the making.

The disciples didn't recognize that Jesus had already given them the clues that victory would be theirs even before their journey began. Jesus told them their journey, no matter what it looked like, was going to be successful when He said; "Let us go to the other side."

The second hint was, "Leaving the crowd behind, they took him along, just as he was, in the boat."

In other words, when Jesus speaks there is no need for any other validations, hesitations, consideration or reservations. It is done! We can take God at His word. I love the fact that word said, "…they took him along, just as he was, in the boat."

This confirmed in my testing all I needed to do was remember who was traveling in my storms with me — Jesus! What was the number one prerequisite I needed to remember while in the storm? "Let us go to the other side." What should my attitude be while traveling through the storm with my passenger by my side? "Leaving the crowd behind, I took him along, just as he was, in my testing."

By understanding when the storms of my life come to rage and the winds begin to bellow, I can rest in the assurance my Redeemer will get up, rebuke the wind and the waves, and command them to "Quiet! Be still!"

And I can simply stand still and watch the victory take its rightful place.

"He was in the world, and the world was made through Him, and the world did not know Him. He came to His own, and those who were His own did not receive Him. But as many as received Him, to them He gave the right to become children of God, even to those who believe in His name."

John 1:11-12 (KJV)

VII. DON'T EXPECT A CROWD TO ATTEND

I honestly don't know of a single person in this world who really wants to go it alone in life. And even if they declare this is true, I have to say I seriously doubt it. Everyone needs company. Not just any company, but the kind that is looking out for you—the people who really truly have your back in a positive way.

In the above scripture, John 1:11-12, we find the words *"He was in the world, and the world was made through Him, and the world did not know Him. He came to His own, and those who were His own did not receive Him."* (KJV) Talk about heartbreak. Those of us how have read our Bibles (even if it is only the gospels) have heard *"In the beginning was the Word and the Word was with God and the Word was God."* John 1:1 (KJV)

We have also been told, read and heard it preached in our ears that Jesus Christ was and is the only true Light of this very dark and dismal world we live in today. And the mere fact John the Baptist was sent to prepare the way for

His arrival deserved everyone's respect and attention to say the least.

Just the sheer fact His presence enlightens us regarding our personal salvation through Him sheds light on those of us who are determined to remain in utter darkness. These words should have been enough.

Yet we find people who were not readily willing to receive Him nor accept the fact He was our answer to salvation and true light to the world.

The truth of the matter was Christ was in the world and he did take upon himself our nature. He dwelled among mankind by His choice. He was

The Son of the Most High, yet he chose on his own recognizance to dwell in the lower part of the world just for you and me.

He was in this world but not of it. He came to save a lost world of which once upon a time, I and trillions of others were a big part of. Quite frankly, until real salvation came to shed light into our darkness, we thought we were living the dream. Nevertheless, we find Christ's willingness to come into an unsavory world to save a lost people, because it was a world of his own creation.

Yet the world did not know, recognize, and could not distinguish who He was. Today there are many who have read about Him, heard about Him, witnessed miracles upon miracles, and yet countless people still don't know Him personally. Others choose not to receive Him or to acknowledge Him as Lord over their lives. Instead, they use phrases like "I was lucky." Or "I accomplished this or that because of my own abilities and smarts."

I am convinced part of the reason why the world does not know Him is because some do not want to part with their sins. Or they need to be in total self-control over their

Living in Purpose

lives, and refuse to surrender their lives. They don't want to put their trust in someone to watch over them and take care of them. They choose to be under their own care, acting as if they can do it better.

One of the sad things about this type of thinking is some people are missing out on such tremendous blessings and breakthroughs for their lives. They are missing the joy and peace our Father wants to bring into their daily lives right now.

But when He returns as Judge, the world will have no other choice but to acknowledge Him for whom he is. We probably all know of someone who says they "know" God. However, there is very little evidence in their daily walk that proves otherwise. Their language does not reflect Christ. Their daily walk bears no indication of him. Their actions are just as revealing now as they were prior to their acceptance of Christ.

When we accept Christ as our Lord and Savior, there should be a desired and noticeable change from some things that are old and familiar to something new and exciting about us. No matter how minute or simple the change or changes may be.

While not comparing myself to the perfection of Christ by any means, it is interesting how life will teach us if we are only willing to pay attention whether in a class or out in our daily surroundings.

What I have noticed now more than ever is we should never overestimate the crowd which is characterized according to Bing dictionary as being a "A large number of persons gathered together; a throng; The common people; the populace. 3. A group of people united by a common cause."

When I think about just how far the Lord has brought

me from certain perspectives and things I used to allow to hold me back from moving forward in the gifts and callings he placed on my life, I honestly cannot help but to throw my head back and laugh out loud.

Just to think, not too long ago, I allowed myself to become overly concerned with being "successful," based upon how many people who would attend my conferences or events as a whole.

I can hardly believe how much energy, time, tears, heartache, thought and even attention I allowed others to take from me when they didn't attend the various conferences.

There were times when I would spend countless hours sending out save the date cards, reminding people to save the date for the conferences. Then I followed it up with personal invitations, and even after that with a personal phone call, text and even an e-blast.

And while some would respond and attend there were others who would see me later and proclaim, "Hello Sister, how was the conference? I have been praying for you." Or "I am sure it went well. I was out of town, busy, the cat ran away, the dog barked and etc...."

Dear God, thank you so very much for the spirit of deliverance in all those areas of my life.

Don't get me wrong. I still wanted people to attend. However, to date, I am more than happy to report I am no longer stressed, overwhelmed, sadden or dismayed if they don't feel the same way about desiring to attend or to support me at all.

I am so very grateful I now know my purpose is not tied to anyone else. It is not based or conditional upon anything else but the Word of God. Today, when I see others struggling with their identities, values or their worth, it makes me weep inside because I can understand their temporary pain. They have not yet come into their truth in God about who they really are, but my prayer for them is they will soon.

Their reactions or the lack of enthusiasm for me used to sometimes dictate my confidence as to whether I believed my events were successful or not. Every now and then, I would be greeted with a question of, "So, who's going to be there?" Or others asked, "Exactly how many people are you expecting to come?" And one of my all- time favorite comments some people would ask was, "Well, let me check my calendar and see what's going on, and I will get back with you. Just know if I am able to make it, I will. If not, know I'm praying for you."

Thank God for a spirit of laughter. Indeed it is a great antidote than medicine. Laughter is said to be the remedy for many sicknesses and health restorations. In fact, HelpGuide.org, cites some of the best health benefits of humor and laughter.

Laughter is good for our health overall because laughter relaxes the whole body by relieving physical tension and stress, leaving our muscles relaxed for up to 45 minutes after. Laughter boosts the immune system by decreasing stress hormones and increases immune cells and infection-fighting antibodies, by improving our resistance to disease.

Laughter also triggers the release of endorphins which is the body's natural feel-good chemicals which promotes overall well-being and can even temporarily relieve pain.

Additionally, laughter protects our hearts by improving the function of blood vessels and increases blood flow, which can help protect us against a heart attack and other cardiovascular problems.

From a physical realm, it has been recognized some of

the benefits of laughter are:
- Boosting our immunity
- Lowering stress hormones
- Decreasing pain
- Relaxing our muscles
- Preventing heart disease

Mental Health Benefits:
- Adds joy and zest to our lives
- Eases anxiety and fear
- Relieves stress
- Improves moods
- Enhances resilience

Some of the social benefits of laughter are:
- Strengthens relationships
- Attracts others to us
- Enhances teamwork
- Helps defuse conflict
- Promotes group bonding
- Laughter dissolves distressing emotions such as feeling anxious, angry, or sad when we are laughing
- Laughter helps keep us relaxed and recharged by reducing stress and increasing energy, enabling us to stay focused and accomplish more
- Laughter and humor shift our perspective allowing us to see situations in a more realistic, less threatening light.

> *"Your sense of humor is one of the most powerful tools you have to make certain that your daily mood and emotional state support good health."*
> ~Paul E. McGhee, PhD ~

The reason for my laugher now is I finally came to the conclusion about three years ago, no one holds the real power to my happiness and joy except me. The real truth of the matter is, I am a survivor whether the whole world supports me or not. My real joy and confidence should never be in questioned based upon others response or reactions to my value or worth.

Coming into this realization and embracing the truth about who God says I am in Him and accepting it in its totality and not just with lip service has brought me to what I call a full circle of living life to its fullest and in the moment.

As a result of this new found revelation, I am now more able to see things differently and through a different set of godly lens that has encouraged me to follow the cloud rather than the unpredictable crowd.

The Bible is an excellent example of crowds. As we know, in Jesus' day everywhere He went He was surrounded by crowds for various reasons. The crowds in some instances symbolized potential disciples who at first expressed a desire to follow Him wherever He went. However, the ultimate question would be whether the crowds stayed with Jesus and become His followers, or turn away and desert him in the end?

Another important aspect I learned about moving forward with purpose is whether it was in my early stages of ministry or during some of the most highlighted times, I had to remain true to myself and what the meaning of my agenda was all about.

I thoroughly enjoy the work of ministry because my heart and soul genuinely love the effort of ministry as a whole. Ministry brings me joy, peace and fullness, and it also inspires me to work in the Kingdom. I am learning daily to work out of my purpose, because it is what moves me to press forward in all I do.

Over time, I have learned not to be moved by crowds or being stroked by people who declare they are with me today. Many times on the next day you cannot locate them even with a tracking system.

> *"Work with enthusiasm, as though you were working for the Lord rather than for people."*
>
> Ephesian 6:7 (NLT)

"But as for me, I trust in You, O LORD, I say, 'You are my God.' My times are in Your hand; Deliver me from the hand of my enemies and from those who persecute me. Make Your face to shine upon Your servant; Save me in Your lovingkindness."

Psalm 31:15-16 (NIV)

VIII. WAIT ON HIM, HE WILL DELIVER ON TIME

In December 2013, I was watching a sermon given by one of my favorite Pastors, Dr. Jazz, and as always, her messages sincerely blessed my heart. Not only does her name identify her, but her specific messages do not fail either.

It does not take a genius to feel her precious Holy Ghost filled spirit through the vibes of the television, IPad, YouTube or what-have-you. Dr. Jazz is something very special.

Anyway, this particular choir was really singing before Dr. Jazz was introduced to preach, and after the singing and an announcement was made for a special offering, the pastor of that church began to introduce Dr. Jazz. During his introduction, the pastor stated he was at another conference in the islands known to great preachers, and he had another pastor in mind to speak that evening.

One of his good friends was also attending the conference and interrupted him and said, "Why don't you ask Dr. Jazz to speak. She is really good and you need to hear her."

He said, "Naw man, I haven't heard of her. I have someone else in mind for this."

Long story short, the friend convinced him to do so and the rest is history.

The part that really caught my attention was now Dr. Jazz was at his church and was the keynote speaker for the evening. But he wanted to make sure everyone realized he was in fact the first person to "discover" her. In short, he was the reason perhaps her ministry exploded to such heights and depths it is today — or so he thought.

I don't know for sure, but I would say perhaps while the pastor's influence played a role in the plan, I would venture further to say God had already predestined the date, time, location, minute and divine connection and everything else relating to Dr. Jazz's debut. Through grace and mercy, he just allowed the pastor to be a part of the bigger picture. Actually, no one gets the glory for that but God.

I am always so energized when I listen to her testimony about the great God she serves. Often in her messages, she shares about her life back in Trinidad, the misfortune of being raped as a young girl and never telling anyone, not even her mother, about it. And now, here it is, years later, God through His incredible timing went to Trinidad and drew her out of seclusion and brought her into her well-lighted season before the masses of all mankind.

He didn't just bring her out, but He alone expedited her timing when the season for her ministry called for her special spiritual anointing. Praise God! He brought her through spiritual doors no earthly chain could hold or bind her back from.

He glided her around naysayers who are still not applauding or cheering her on, but that's okay, because when God calls, there is no one in the crowd who can silence the voice of thunder.

I have to believe that as God continues to deliver and keep Dr. Jazz, He is still closing doors that are no longer necessary or needful to remain open as she passes through. When she preaches, I can sense Jesus is with her. It's as though she is transported to another dimension. Her face lights up, and her disposition explodes upon contact as though she has collided with a force much greater than she.

To me, she is an excellent example of what it means to wait upon God, allowing Him to preserve, prepare and protect me from all harm and danger.

After witnessing Dr. Jazz minister, I know God definitely knows how to groom me for His vineyard as well as His courtyard of grace. So when the timing is right for my life, gift and purpose to come forth, He alone will propel me forward and upward where I will surely reap the tremendous harvest He has promised to me.

The will to wait, rest, depend and lean on God is a force to be reckoned with and a stance not to be entered into lightly. In fact, the art of waiting can almost drive some people to the brink of insanity and force them to make decisions irrationally outside of the will and parameter of God's intended purpose for their lives.

In my own life I am finding out each and every day what it means to truly "wait" upon the Lord. Not just wait, but to be in expectation with good cheer and not being filled with anxiety and anxiousness for when God will show up.

For some the thought may seem simple and readily easy to ascertain. However, once the process is in pursuit and the timeframe from when God said it until the time of manifestation has transpired, that's when the pressure begins mounting up, and unfortunately, the doubt and the doubters start showing up. This is also the time when one has to dig their heels in and declare, "Lord I trust Your word over my life."

Recently, I began to challenge myself to monitor those specific moments when they occur in my life. The first thing I began to do was trace my thinking and write down what I was dwelling on the most. The second process for me was to trace my emotions in the waiting.

In other words, did the anxiousness come from outside pressures or from the inside of me wanting to know the "exactness" of when everything was going to work out for my good?

I followed this process for about a month. When I went back to review my notes I must say, there it was in black and white. One of the most startling things I remembered most about my experience was everything I had written down had to do with "my expectations and timeframes." Most of my requests did not leave much room for God to work on my behalf.

Without a written history I could use to measure or reflect back to about my past behavior as it related to my anxiousness, I am sure I would have continued business as usual, relating to my outward expectations. Choose to wait on God, because we know firsthand He will deliver us on time.

> *"You are my God. My times are in Your hand; Deliver me from the hand of my enemies and from those who persecute me. Make Your face to shine upon Your servant; Save me in Your lovingkindness."*
>
> Psalms 118:28 (NIV)

"I will lead the blind by ways they have not known, along unfamiliar paths I will guide them; I will turn the darkness into light before them and make the rough places smooth. These are the things I will do; I will not forsake them."

Isaiah 42:16 (NIV)

IX. COMFORT IN HIS NAME

Facing difficulties is never easy for anyone at any time, no matter how prayed up and fortified we would like to believe we are. A trial is a trial is a trial on a good day. And nothing but the grace and absolute mercies of God can guide us through and keep us while we are in the eye of the storm. Nothing but the incredible name of Jesus!

Most of us don't even have a clue a storm is brewing. At least not unless and until we see the horrific clouds hovering over our heads, or we recognize the sun has suddenly disappeared from the sky and is hidden behind the clouds. Even then we may not sense danger immersing the world all around us.

Prior to that, we've never stopped and paid attention long enough to notice all day long or even perhaps for a while, the clouds have been formulating for quite a while, especially during the times we have not been paying attention to our surroundings.

Sometimes, by the time we decide to look up and pay attention to what is hurtling around us, it's too late. Not only have the clouds formulated, but at any minute, they are heavy with precipitation. It looks like the clouds could give way at any moment, and we all know what it is like to get caught up in a really bad, unsuspected storm at what seemed to be the last minute. We are ill-prepared to move forward and/or find suitable shelter.

Just reading the Scripture He will lead the "blind by ways they have not known" is enough to make me run in the spirit realm when nothing is chasing after me.

I know what it is like to find myself halted between two opinions or decisions and not having the wherewithal to make what I call an intelligent decision between the two. That's a very uncomfortable, uneasy, unrestful place and position to be in.

You know the type of decision making you have to do when you find yourself straddle between "pressure" and "confusion" and "stress" is only feet away. Doubt is gaining on you fast and all you can think of is "which way must I go?" Sadly enough, there have been days in my life when I found myself between natural rocks and in need of a spiritual decision, but I was too "afraid" to decide on either. It is not a good place to be.

But thanks be to the Lord of Lord and Kings of Kings, one day I found myself immersed in Scripture reading when I happened upon Psalm 46:1-10.

> *"God is our refuge and strength,*
>   *an ever-present help in trouble.*
> *Therefore we will not fear, though the earth give way*
>   *and the mountains fall into the heart of the sea,*
>   *though its waters roar and foam*
>   *and the mountains quake with their surging.*
> *There is a river whose streams make glad the city*

of God,
*   the holy place where the Most High dwells.*
God is within her, she will not fall;
*   God will help her at break of day.*
Nations are in uproar, kingdoms fall;
*   he lifts his voice, the earth melts.*
The LORD Almighty is with us;
*   the God of Jacob is our fortress.*
Come and see what the LORD has done,
*   the desolations he has brought on the earth.*
He makes wars cease
*   to the ends of the earth.*
He breaks the bow and shatters the spear;
*   he burns the shields with fire.*
He says, "Be still, and know that I am God. (NIV)

When I read down to the word "trouble," the Spirit of the Lord began to deal with me about that word "trouble," which caused me to investigate a little deeper. He allowed me to see it meant He is the God who is able to handle me and my situations when I find myself in life's "tight" spots.

Tight spots for me are those times when life troubles, pressures, trials and tribulations come to oppress and depress me at the same exact time. Tight spots are the moments when issues and life circumstances seem to attempt to fence me in and buffet me on every side. They come to confirm there is no real way out of this current trial.

It is in those moments when the "tight spots" make every attempt to squeeze every ounce of joy and strength within me out to make sure I cave and buckle underneath the earthly weight of it all. However, I am learning to continuously call upon the name of Jesus, because I found when I do so, He is that God who is the lifter of my head and the supplier of my every conceivable need.

He is the One who is more than able to do in me and for me exceedingly, abundantly above all I can think or image. He is able to set my foot on a solid rock. He is able to turn every one of my midnights into day. He is not just a burden barrier, but He is also a heavy load carrier. He doesn't just break every chain but He is more than able to destroy every yoke and send it packing for good.

"I will lead the blind by ways they have not known, along unfamiliar paths I will guide them;"

Not only does the Scripture boast about God being able to lead the blind by ways we have not known, along unfamiliar paths, He will guide us as well. This is enough to make me shout right in my tracks.

The enemy of this world is used to causing pains, discords, distractions, upheavals and challenges in our daily lives. From time-to-time, willingly or unwillingly, we occasionally fall prey to his evil devices through word and/or deed. Sometimes it can be both when we are not really focusing on what we are giving our attention to.

That being said, we can count on the enemy knowing the number one way to gain yardage on the people of God is to keep us "distracted" away from the Word of God and unfocused on what really matters most. Usually when this takes place, our guards are down and so are our defenses. We can become the "weakest link" in our own journeys to victory, and little do we know, that's when he moves in for the silent kill.

Knowing the Scripture just said "He will lead the blind by ways they have not known; along "unfamiliar" paths I will guide them" should give us a sense of solace, knowing we have absolutely nothing to fear. No matter the trial or situation, our God is pro us.

In other words, God's ways are never old, stale, same-old, same-old. We will never be able to "know" all of Him and figure Him out in one scenario. His ways are not our ways. All we need do is trust Him completely. God has already gotten us the victory through His Son Jesus Christ, and nothing and no one can change His mind toward us.

While the enemy of this world is trying desperately to destroy our testimonies, confuse our minds and sow discord in and through our lives, God has already fought every battle and begotten for us the victory through our Lord and Savior. He devised a plan so authentic even the devil in hell doesn't know about it. And we cannot figure it out.

When it comes to why we go through difficult and challenging times, the Bible doesn't offer an exhaustive amount of information as to why we have trouble and trials. We can all conclude certain explanations as to why some things happen, but there seems to be more questions than answers, which can often leave us frustrated, jilted, wounded and sometimes bitter in the aftermath of it all.

It is within those restless moments we cannot process the pain, the rejection or the disappointments. That is the time we must trust God with ourselves and know He is a Good Shepherd, highly qualified to meet and super-exceed all of our needs at the same time if necessary.

For me, learning how to take each day and focus my attention in the Word of God helps me grow while I am in what I call life's "challenging moments." I learned how to hold my head up instead of down, bemoaning my temporary, according to the bible, "light afflictions."

Though at times, the weight of my burdens appears very difficult and situations sometimes are extremely strenuous. When my focus moves to the Word of God and not my personal situation, I know for myself, God alone is more than able to supply my every need—even before I ask or call upon Him.

"Praise be to the God and Father of our Lord Jesus Christ, the Father of compassion and the God of all comfort, who comforts us in all our troubles, so that we can comfort those in any trouble with the comfort we ourselves receive from God. For just as the sufferings of Christ flow over into our lives, so also through Christ our comfort overflows." 2 Corinthians 1:3-5 (CSB)

Not only is He a God who cares about us, but He is the Father of compassion and the God of all comfort. He is able to turn each and every one of our midnights into days—not after the storm passes over, but while it is working against us and is in full force.

The word comfort means to soothe, console, or reassure; bring cheer to. He is indeed a God of great comfort. He takes pleasure in taking care of us in every aspect of our lives. He takes care to heal our wounds and make us whole again after every hurt and pain. He is a faithful God of love, grace and mercy.

The comfort we find in the Name of Jesus is like none other in the world. In fact, He is whatever we need in the moment. Though the basic concept, the word comfort means to ease, give relief, help, cheer up, exhort, and fear not. We find in the Old and New Testaments the word "comfort" is encouragement, whether it's by word or His presence around us when we find ourselves in need of being comforted.

When we grasp just how much ammunition and spiritual power is unleashed in the incredible name of Jesus on our behalf, it causes all the fears from our temporary light afflicts to simply disintegrate at a twinkling of an eye.

Our God is indeed more than enough and more than we can ever need in this lifetime. His Name trumps all and is irreplaceable over anything and anyone. There is absolutely none like Him in all the earth.

Daily I am trying more to watch what I call my "daily intake" and my "outlet." I realize my natural eyes serve as portals that will allow certain worldly data to enter and flow through my decision making devices. If I am unaware of what penetrates through the filters of my natural sight at lightning record speeds, I will soon become inundated with all sorts of mishaps and bad decision making, simply based upon my emotions and feelings with nothing based upon the true Word of God.

In order for me to be successful and rest in the comforts of God's peace, I must saturate my life and my daily walk with the Word of God. There are countless ways of doing so. However, nothing trumps prayer and meditation upon who He is according to my faith and belief in His word. I believe there is no other name I can pronounce that triumphs over the name of Jesus no matter what.

In other words, we must take care to remember our God is the God of all comfort: In fact, according to Isaiah 51:12, the word of God declares that: "*I, even I, am he who comforts you.*" Additionally, in Isaiah 51:3 and Isaiah 51:19, God is not only the creator God who consoles, but he comes in time of calamity and gives help.

According to BibleStudyTools.com, The gospel is given in Isaiah 40:1, where he exhorts, "*Comfort, comfort my people, says your God.*" The final twenty-six chapters of Isaiah are often called "*the volume of comfort*" with its promise of present comfort and the future promise of the suffering servant who comes to give hope, help, and release to comfort all who mourn. (See Isaiah 61:3.)

The command of Moses to not be afraid (Exodus 14:13; 20:20) is a command intended to bring comfort to the people.

Isaiah intends to bring comfort as he echoes God's presence among his people.

I am so very grateful the name of God is richness that is forever unfolding daily right before our spiritual eyes. He is never just one given thing, but rather His name is vast and unlimited in all His ways.

He is unlimited, all knowing, everlasting, the beginning and our ending. He is without fail. In Isaiah 51:12; 2 Corinthians 1:3, He is considered as the ***author of comfort***, and Christ is the comforter, intercessor and advocate for us all. In my very humble opinion, it doesn't get any better than that.

Knowing this, we can be free to move ahead in the specific promises God has aligned for our individual lives, which is incredible. Being fully persuaded, influenced, converted, confident and assured that whatever it is our God has assigned our hands to do in the great work of the Kingdom, He has already prepared us and ordained us to get it accomplished.

Yes, we can expect pop-ups from the enemy at every turn along the way but if God has already pronounced a blessing on it, the enemy cannot run ahead of it and call it cursed. God's Word overrules every single time, no matter whom or what is attempting to oppose it. We can still go forth and conqueror in Jesus' name.

SECTION THREE

"Cast your burden upon the LORD and He will sustain you; He will never allow the righteous to be shaken"

Psalm 55:22

X. SOUL CARETAKER

A soul caretaker is one who ministers to the totality of the body, soul and the mind of a person. This expression reminds me of the Alka-Seltzer commercial. Once the Alka-Seltzer is released against its target's goal, which is the water, it starts to react and respond by fizzling and releasing tiny sparkles everywhere into the water.

On contact, there is absolutely no turning back once the purpose has begun. After the product has been digested, it is designed to go to work immediately upon contact of the main inner problem, which is the digestive system, and rid the individual of indigestion issues and assist with any blockage that may be causing any discomfort.

The role of a true soul caretaker is to carefully aide and assist the individual they are caring for, well-rounded in their daily affairs regardless of what those needs are. The soul caretaker's primary role is to make sure their assignment in that individual's life is met according to the role and agreement of care being assigned to their hands to do. This role is a tremendous responsibility that should never be entered into lightly and certainly without prayer and supplication.

The soul caretaker is careful in going the extra step in

providing what is relevant and significant to the individual's needs they are caring for and imparting into the life of another. To make sure their overall benefit is in complete alignment with the will, purpose and plan of God for that individual's life.

While caretaking or caregiving is never an "easy" and light-hearted responsibility, it can be a very rewarding and promising role for that individual who really has a godly heart to serve in that capacity.

It can be rewarding to serve others whom God has called that individual to and to know the difference between being used by others and serving them as God has called them to do. A soul caretaker's role or work is not done unto man but unto God.

Should you encounter a conversation with most caretakers today, the ones who serve and those who have served diligently in some capacity in the past as a soul caretaker, they will tell you one of the main reasons for doing so was because they loved the individual they took care of.

They never came to the duty with an ulterior motive other than because of love. They didn't serve out of money or bragging rights or even to be noticed by others. They choose to serve out of a sense of love and caring. And above all, they believed they were commissioned by God to serve others first.

A soul caretaker is not one that serves under duress or pressure to "serve" but one that goes willingly to do so. They serve no matter what time of day or night, whether someone is watching or not. Most real caretakers are not even remotely paid for the level of care they provide to others. This type of care in fact is "priceless."

They truly serve out of their heart and soul. My mother

was such a person. In my early years of growing up, our family faithfully watched and participated in the assistance of our mother taking care of her mother to a fault.

Our mother served out of gladness and with a very humble humanitarian spirit. She served her mother before, during and even after a long day at work and taking care of her family. I don't think my mother knew what a work shift really was.

There were many times Mom could be counted upon after leaving work and not even stopping to catch her breath before moving on to the next assignment concerning her mother's well-being. As a child, I don't believe there were many moments my mother didn't have her mother on her mind in some manner. In fact, she was always looking for things that would or could make my grandmother's life easier.

She wasn't paid and never even thought of asking for pay. That was her beloved mother, and nothing or no certain amount of money was going to keep her away from attending to her every need, no matter what. My mother worked tirelessly to make sure her mother was warm, dry, fed and comfortable.

Grandmother and Mom loved each other deeply. There was something about knowing once upon a time my grandmother took care of my mother as a child. Then it was my mother's turn to embrace and accept the opportunity and willingness to return the favor when she didn't really have to, but she choose to do so out of real love and respect for her mother.

Without fail, Mom could often be found serving even when she had another sibling living practically in the house with our grandmother but wouldn't necessarily lift a finger to do much—unless you count picking up the phone to dial for others to come and assist. Anyway, our mother would go to her regular job, come home and take care of her immediate family members.

Next, she would take one of the children and walk approximately fourteen miles one way because we didn't have a car. Mother never worried about how she was going to get to her mother, because she always relied upon God for help and His direction.

There was never, ever any doubt about how my mother felt about her mom. You could see the love miles and miles away. Daily, Mother only slowed down between routines long enough to catch her breath and give us chore assignments. Then out the door she would go.

From the moment she reached her mom's place, she entered the door preparing to take care of her mother's personal needs, change her bedding and feed her. Quite often, as the case may have been, her mother would not have been changed, feed or seen after all day by anyone else, especially those that lived closed by.

It didn't matter if it was late at night or early in the morning. Mother served her mother with gladness. She exhibited love as only God would do for each of us. She didn't pass the buck—she didn't summon others. She didn't get on the phone and talk to her siblings about what a poor job they were doing. She just served with gladness.

The day our grandmother passed away, I was there with her. She and I were talking and having so much fun. I remember my grandmother was in the middle of telling me a funny story, and my other aunt was present as well. All of a sudden, my grandmother was laughing and simply turned her head and stared far away, as if she was looking at something amazing. Then she drew her last breath.

My mother had only left for a few hours to go wash my

grandmother's clothes. She asked me to stay with my grandmother while she was away. I was often very nervous to do so because my grandmother was notorious for seeing dead people in the spirit and talking with them out loud.

It was never considered strange for my grandmother to carry on a conversation with you, and all of a sudden she would say something like this to her deceased husband. "What are you doing here? Can't you see me talking right now? I will be home shortly, just wait." With that comment, she would turn around and say to me, "Okay, child, now what was I saying?"

Little did she know, I really wanted to say, "Grandma please tell me that while you were speaking to him he was nowhere near me." Honestly, in that moment, I couldn't even feel my own pulse nor my heartbeat. The mere fact my grandmother and grandfather were carrying on a conversation in my presence like nobody's business was more than I could handle.

I was too afraid to stay and too scared to run away because of the noted consequences I would have undoubtedly received upon my mother's return. Once I thought about it, perhaps listening to a personal conversation between the dead and the living might not have been so bad after all, especially when I thought about the alternative.

Now where was I, oh yeah, sitting at the end of my grandmother's bed. While in the middle of laughing at the funny story she was telling me, my grandmother just tilted her head and with a smile on her face, she simply laughed on away with ease. I noticed the change immediately.

However, to my surprise, on the other hand, my aunt had no earthly idea her beloved mother had just slipped away in her presence. I was extremely hesitant to even say anything, because I knew my auntie was a very nervous person who did not deal well with surprises at all. Nevertheless, I had no choice but to tell her. It didn't go over too well.

When our mother returned from the laundromat, I met her halfway and told her the news her beloved mother had just passed away but not before asking for her pet name she had always called Mother.

"Where is Red?" My grandmother asked. Even on her deathbed, a soul caretaker bond can be ever so connected and threaded with pure love.

A soul caretaker is very much involved in the overall grand scheme of things. They are not standoffishness. They are never in a rush all the time. And they are not acting in the role of a caregiver begrudgingly.

They are always nearby and productive while serving. They are present and very much in the moment. They are intercessors and providers, covenant keepers, soul stirrers and godly advocates for those they serve.

Soul caretakers are what I believe are divinely connected by faith, love and true diligence. They serve within their range of purpose and call. They work out of their specified assignment according to the will of God for their lives. My oldest sister Pearlie is that kind of person. In my opinion, she is the definition of "servant."

For as long as I can remember growing up, well before I even knew how to spell such a word, she was the epitome of servanthood—perhaps because she had seen it being done before her very eyes.

Personally, sometimes especially in my younger years, I felt as though she served some individuals who quite frankly used and abused her kindness and her sincerity to her detriment. But I have no doubt, God will reward her for the kindness she showed to many others.

Another important note about being a soul caretaker is they must possess the willingness and faithfulness to serve unselfishly according to God's plan and purpose for their lives. Their work must be credited unto God and not for their own glory or mankind's notice.

If a soul caretaker's role is anything other than a calling, it is more than likely a career choice that often doesn't pay much. I can assure you, true soul caretakers are not in it for earthly pay, if I may say so myself. If an individual was trying to accomplish this goal on their own, and in their own strength, not only would this not make a good career choice for them, but it wouldn't last long either.

The true role for a soul caretaker is priceless and often faceless, because they are not necessarily high profile positions, and no one really appreciates a caretaker until they find themselves in need of one.

When I think of soul caretakers, there are other persons which come to mind. My siblings Dorothy and Eddie. Wow! These are two individuals who didn't have a motive for any other purpose but to simply serve. They were there for my husband and me in every conceivable way when we could not do for ourselves. They were our hands and our feet. No jobs were too insignificant, and no jobs were too overbearing.

Daily Audie and I witnessed on different levels their desire to serve and render aide of any kind, and they each did it with gladness. I thank our God for their precious servanthood.

Someone may say, "Oh well, yes, they are your brother and sister. They should have."

Audie and I say, "True, they are family. But family, just like others, are not necessarily obligated to help just because help is needful."

I am a firm believer to really serve requires a God-given servant's heart.

Let's ask the Word of God about what it has to say about "servanthood." The answers just might surprise you. We will find the Bible has a lot to say about servanthood, because the Bible is considered the central headquarters of what true authentic servanthood is all about. Why? Because Jesus Christ was the chief of all servants.

"For even the Son of Man did not come to be served, but to serve, and to give His life a ransom for many." Mark 10:45 (NIV) When we give Jesus Christ His rightful place as Lord of our lives, His lordship will be expressed in the way we serve others. (Mark 9:35; 1 Peter 4:10; John 15:12-13) www.Got Questions.org

I am learning each day of my life, servanthood is not something talked about but rather demonstrated through my daily actions and not my knee-jerked reaction.

Servanthood is a calling birthed out of compassion, grace and mercy and covered with the willingness to serve others first. As my friend Cynthia always says, "It ain't for the faint hearted." In fact, it is one of the most unselfish acts of godly kindness that can ever be shown to another.

"For what we preach is not ourselves, but Jesus Christ as Lord, with ourselves as your servants for Jesus' sake." 2 Corinthians 4:5 (NIV)

I am still surprised even to this day when I encounter ministers and preachers of whom I have had personal conversations with who still think in some strange arbitrary way, it is all about them as it relates to the pulpit or handing out assignments.

They just don't seem to understand God can and will use whom He very well pleases, and He does not need the nod or amen from others to make His choice known to mankind.

For some leaders it is quite evident they thoroughly enjoy preaching on Sundays but may not see the need to execute what is being preached through the work week. I have had frank conversations with some who really believe they are only called to study and "preach" the gospel to others.

They sometimes think going to the hospitals and ministering to the homeless or others is someone else's job to handle. While in the very beginning of their call from the Lord, there may have been great excitement. However, over time, there appears to be a disconnection between what the full charge of ministry entails.

To me, all of ministry is vital. There should not be any part of ministry that is off limits unto the Lord. We should possess a willing attitude and I can do personality to the will and flow of God's purpose in our lives.

True leadership is servanthood one-on-one, and the greatest leader of all time is Jesus Christ. Servanthood is an attitude exemplified by Christ *"who, though he was in the form of God, did not count equality with God a thing to be grasped, but emptied himself, taking the form of a servant."* Philippians 2:6-7 (ESV) Even today, our Lord and Savior still serves humanity in every capacity and has continued to do so from the beginning of time.

Certainly this is not the case for everyone in the world today. However, to some, the very thought of being asked to serve is almost like asking them to do the unthinkable out loud.

Live and recorded media to practically every so-called reality show demonstrates to the umpteen powers their "right" to be served in every possible way based upon their

Living in Purpose

materialistic lifestyle and man-made self-stardom.

For the most part, the image they portray themselves as is a horrifying sight to say the least. From the blatant disrespect they readily unleash on each person who does not readily agree with whatever ideas are to the mere thought someone else within their camp holds themselves up to a different standard than they do.

It is so sad these shows are willing to display to the world their need for superficial control, material things and their version of "success" or what it means to be "successful." Through watching these shows it is clear to see some of the "realities" of certain shows is everything but. More than likely, during the shows, the reality stars very rarely if ever display a servanthood mentality, let alone a servant lifestyle toward others at all.

Most of these people would say they are Christians and they believe in Jesus, but from the looks of things via their various shows and display of their versions of reality, it can be viewed as polar opposite of what the Bible actually teaches or honors today.

The five words in the New Testament translated "ministry" generally refer to servanthood or service given in love. Serving others is the very essence of ministry. All believers are called to ministry (Matthew 28:18-20), whether it is from a pulpit or not, on the street corner or in a prison camp. The location really doesn't matter. Therefore, we are all called to be servants for the glory of God. Living is giving—all else is selfishness and boredom.

I believe as we continue to live in a world that is forever evolving, our nation and world system is going to become surrounded by a greater need for soul caretakers to assist with the tremendous woes and catastrophic atrocities of our nation.

In the coming years, it is going to be imperative for those individuals to understand the importance of learning how to look around and ask God for direction on how to serve others beyond their own family and friends network.

They'll need to know how to reach out and help someone else when they are in need without cameras rolling or being taped before a live studio audience. It doesn't matter whether the need is great or small, help is help in the simplest form.

Soul caretaking is a privileged position that for the most part is not coveted, glamorous or necessarily a high profile role. It is, however, a position of true servanthood filled with grace, dignity, humanness, kindness and godly love. It serves without color, expectancy or payback by man.

Caretaking can be a unique way in which to give back to someone. It is an opening to pour back into the life of another who may or may not know Jesus Christ, and through our kindness and compassion, His light in us can shine through for others to see. It is a chance to win souls for the kingdom and perhaps make a true friend in the process.

It has been rightly stated, "Rank is given you to enable you to better serve those above and below you. It is not given for you to practice your idiosyncrasies." (General Bruce C. Clarke, USA, Ret)

Let's serve others by serving Christ (Colossians 3:23-24). God the Father has served us by sacrificing Christ on the cross for our sins, and we should serve others by giving the gospel and our lives to them (1 Thessalonians 1:5-6). Those who desire to be great in God's kingdom must be the servant of all (Matt 20:26).

"Many are the plans in the mind of a man, but it is the purpose of the Lord that will stand."

Proverbs 19:21 (ESV)

XI. HIS PURPOSE IS IN HIS PROMISE

While sitting in our weekly Wednesday mid-day Bible study class one day, a gentleman made a statement. "If you wanna make God laugh, all we have to do is present Him with our daily plans." Not only did his statement grab my attention, I thought to myself, "Wow, how true is that?"

It is true—man labors day in and day out trying to figure out from one minute to the next what his life will entail. We make plans as far out as years in advance about things we are going to do, sometimes never stopping to think about what God may have to say about any of it. We ignore the fact we will need his guidance, support, wisdom and strength to make any of it happen.

Rather, we just start planning with our own personal agendas in mind and think God has no other choice but to go alone with whatever we say about our lives. All we need for Him to do is show up and endorse them without questioning our motives at all. How mistaken can we be? Our God deserves and desires so much more from us, for starters. He wants to be included in all things.

The Word of God explicitly says in Proverbs 19:21, "Many are the plans in the mind of a man, but it is the purpose of the Lord that will stand." Clearly He leaves no doubt about what we can expect and whose guidelines we must adhere to. Mankind will never, ever run anything. God is consistently in control over it all. And I for one am very thankful it is so.

My life stands as a personal testament you will need and should always choose for God to be at the helm of all of life's choices. When Scripture states we can do nothing without God, those words could not be more accurate or surreal. Try as we might to operate without Him, we find nothing from nothing leaves absolutely less than what we originally started out with.

I strongly believe God always has a plan for everything He does. We don't necessarily know or grasp what that particular plan is aside from God's wisdom. But, God does, and in his perfect timing alone, He will reveal it. The only problem with that is, we are not necessarily the most patient people.

Most of the time we like to be made aware of the going-on as quickly as possible, absolutely with no mystery at all — so we can hurry up and stress, become frustrated and irritated in the meantime until we see the complete fruition of it all.

Not fully grasping the fact it is God alone who said, "For He knows the thoughts that He thinks towards us." So if we continue to stress and wear ourselves out about the process and the plan beforehand, by the appropriate time when the manifestation of the plan has appeared, we are in no physical and sometimes spiritual condition to even begin the labor it requires to finish it.

Within ourselves, we do not possess the patience necessary to "wait" and to be trained, prepared or have the maturity to grow into that purpose God has for us. We must learn there is in fact a discipline, order and molding that goes into our purpose.

We cannot wake up one day and dive headfirst into what we think we ought to do without any godly direction, wisdom, knowledge or resources to get it done. This to me is called being led and operating in the arm of the flesh.

Have you ever dealt with a person who had big dreams, ideas and even perhaps goals? Each and every time they spoke about them, their vision sounded interesting and intriguing enough. However, there was just one problem — they didn't have any resources or connections to make them happen.

Have you ever met someone with all the ambition in the world, but they depended upon others to supply the resources, location and even the marketing to make their "dreams" come true? So when they come to you for the resources or connections (the hook-ups) to bring their desires into fruition, they become somewhat disgruntled and perhaps even angry and bewildered with you because you didn't comply with their wishes.

Most often that's how we operate in our walk with Christ. We acknowledge Him as Savior of our eternity but not Lord over our lives on Earth. For some, that may be looked upon as being an invasion of privacy that's no one else's business but theirs and perhaps a little too close for comfort. In a roundabout way, it's like, I'll call you if I need your type of relationship.

Here's my concern with all of that. Our desires, plans, purposes and dreams should never stop or be reduced to the hands of mankind. It is a wonderful thing to have others support us, encourage us, and even listen to our heart's desire. Still, all of those plans should be left in the hands of our Amazing and Almighty God alone.

There is absolutely no way mankind can ever know the

true plans and purpose for our existence or the entirety of our call on Earth. Therefore, we never should attempt to allow someone else to practice or predict the outcome of our dreams on us in any shape, form or fashion.

Mankind simply does not and cannot provide us with the wherewithal for anything. Through regular common sense or their own personal head knowledge no one can perceive what truly the "best" is for anyone, including in their own lives.

It takes an Almighty God to do Almighty things. He is the only one who is more than able to set our lives and our livelihoods into order from the beginning until the end. He is the only one who is able to define destinies and our purposes according to what the Kingdom needs.

I believe our God is far more interested in building His people up with believers who will take Him at His word and through our living win more souls for the Kingdom of God. I believe God desires for us to become more and more Kingdom minded before His return for the benefit of winning souls.

Not fully understand prophesy, I can remember earlier in my younger Christian life, as soon as there was a prophetic word spoken over me about the tiniest glimpse of purpose I thought, "Well where is it? Shouldn't it be here by now?" I was thinking shouldn't I be in receipt of the gift, strength, wisdom, knowledge and the ability to start operating in that purpose like yesterday?

We run ahead of the vision without every grasping the provision, the sound instructions and sometimes even the anointing to accomplish the task. There are times when there is the necessary means through provision to move forward, but we don't possess the maturity to carry the vision to full term because we get distracted along the way.

While Proverbs 19:21 declares *"many are the plans in the mind of a man, but it is the purpose of the Lord that will stand,"* that lets me know it is not just about "planning" my way that must take place. Other vital roles and preparation must be brought to the table as well. Consider the following things that need to happen as part of moving forward.

Strategic Planning:

Without an objective and unbiased understanding of "what the purpose is, we're not likely to come up with strategies that will cause the purpose to be very effective. Before a career is taken on, a ministry is established, a business venture is decided, a marriage takes place or what-have-you, we owe it to ourselves to take a hard look at what's happening externally and internally. We must pay special attention to the needs of others involved or to whom it will affect. As John Dewey once said, "A problem well defined is a problem half solved."

Clarity of purpose and realistic goals

Even when God has given us a specific promise in his Word, there is still what I call "spiritual details" that must be worked out or considered. Many people assume they can skip the preliminaries and go right into the purpose, deciding to very deliberately overlook the purpose, which is the part where we get to take personal ownership, accountability and labor in bringing the purpose into fruition through our obedience to the plan of God.

Waiting is a work in progress. It takes enormous patience and diligence to wait and trust God for the promise. It's critical in the meantime to understand the purpose of strategic initiative and to have clear goals that are aspirational, yet realistic. We must understand God is not going to do it all for us. We have a role and a part to plan in the purpose and the plan as well.

Ned Frey, owner of Foursight Seminars Inc., talks about this subject in terms of "purpose, focus and passion." Clarity of purpose fuels the focus and passion required to achieve a sustainable, successful effort. In other words, while God has a purpose for our lives, we still need to show up for the plan and possess humbleness and a grateful spirit He included for us in the plan.

Sense of urgency

Romans 12:11 tells us, *"Never be lazy, but work hard and serve the Lord enthusiastically."* (NLT)

"Without a sense of urgency, it's too easy to put off until tomorrow what should be acted upon today," says Allen Hauge, president of Hauge Farms, Inc. Harvard Business School professor.

Emeritus John Kotter describes it as "a gut level determination to act today."

It doesn't mean lighting a fire under someone by manipulating urgency through false crisis. Instead, it's about lighting the fire within and inspiring a sustainable will to change.

Strategies that underscore our values and Matters to the Kingdom Building

Strategy, as it relates to the preparation of the purpose and the plan God has for our lives, isn't just about what anyone would do. It's about understanding what WE would do, based on our priorities and values to the purpose and plan God has called us to do and in the timeframe in which He has released the plan for our lives to be accomplished.

In Romans 12:11, each of us are charged to carry out the

work of the Kingdom with urgency and to diligently pursue our callings for the work of the Kingdom for ourselves as well our families. We must not become satisfied with becoming complacent or lazy in our duty to serve God.

As a people of God it is imperative we should diligently pursue our official callings—whether it is preaching, teaching, praying, reading or whatever forms of ministry and/or corporate businesses God has called us to. Do it with a sense of reverence.

We must be ready and willing to move forward to every good work, and particularly, that which may be greatly designed for us to carry out. Ministering to the poor saints in their necessity, in which we show kindness, tenderness, affection and brotherly love, at the end of the day, we must be quick to give that honor and respect to whom it is due—back to God.

Understanding Whose Purpose It Is

We must never lose sight of whose purpose the plan is designed for in the first place. As a people of God we are excited about the purpose God has bestowed on us. Sometimes, we temporarily forget what the original intent of the plan started out to be, or we forget its Originator. The purpose was never about us. Nor was it ever intended to be. And until we do it God's way, the purpose will never work successfully.

Leadership Is a Major Part of His Purpose

John 13:16 states, *"I tell you the truth, slaves are not greater than their master. Nor is the messenger more important than the one who sends the message."* (NLT) Basically speaking, we must be prepared to follow the Leader at all times. There are absolutely, no short cuts or variations from the original plan.

Jesus has already modeled the way, and now we must follow our leader where He leads us. Even though all the above mention has been good, it is still not enough if we are to carry out the purpose and plan God has for our lives successfully.

Unwavering Discipline

Commitment to achieving strategic goals as it relates to purpose is still not enough—we also need execution. Successful execution means having the discipline necessary to achieve our goals and make sustainable behavioral change.

In individual terms, for example, someone might be committed to starting a brand new business. Yet he or she may lack the discipline to do what's necessary to achieve that goal and maintain the new skillset and self-control to show up for work on time, even if they are the boss. It's no different in ministry.

Transparency

Honesty is essential if we are to reap the many benefits and blessings of seeing the plan and purpose for our lives come into fruition. We must embrace the strategic plan as our plan by taking pride and due diligence to the steps that are being laid out before us. Lacking discipline, humility, faithfulness and gratitude l for the things God is providing to us so we will be a success is just asking for failure.

Transparency with God is always a major step. For one, He already knows our strengths and weaknesses. Remember, He did not call the equipped, but rather equips those He calls. So in order to accomplish this level of success, it's important to have transparency right from the start.

Monitoring, Measurement and Feedback

Once again, "Many are the plans in the mind of a man, but it is the purpose of the Lord that will stand." No matter how great we may deem our personal purpose or plan, it will never sway or change the heart of our Almighty God. Therefore, it is incumbent upon us to always look to Jesus, who is the author and the finisher of our faith for direction at all times. We should never attempt to go it alone.

"Even the best strategic plans require adjustments along the way," says Linda Gabbard, president of Framework Initiatives Company, Inc. That means looking at both intended and unintended effects.

Monitor our plan's progress. Measure outputs as well as outcomes. Obtain feedback from those who have our best interest at heart, genuinely love us and stay in our corner. Identifying and documenting key critiquing about the plan is essential, as well as periodically, challenging our assumptions. If the assumptions are no longer relevant, our plan won't be either.

Anchoring the changes in company culture

"Who dares despise the day of small things, since the seven eyes of the LORD that range throughout the earth will rejoice when they see the chosen capstone in the hand of Zerubbabel?" Zechariah 4:10 (NIV)

Recognizing small wins and victories are exciting at any stage in our journeys. If we continue to remain faithful to the plan set before us, God promises us in His Word we reap if we faint not. A reward from our Heavenly Father produces a sense of reinforcement and a step in the right direction for us. Being grateful will go a long way in taking strategy and change from what we do to being who we are in Christ.

> "It is better to lead from behind and to put others in front, especially when you celebrate victory when nice things occur. You take the front line when there is danger. Then people will appreciate your leadership."
>
> Nelson Mandela

XII. HE IS A MIGHTY GOOD LEADER

Psalms 24:7-9 declares the Lord as being Mighty and also describes the earth as being the Lord's. We are encouraged to *"Lift up your heads, O gates, and be lifted up, O ancient doors that the King of glory may come in! Who is the King of glory? The LORD strong and mighty, The LORD mighty in battle. Lift up your heads, O gates, and lift them up, O ancient doors, that the King of glory may come in!"* (KJV)

There was a particular song my grandmother used to sing. It encouraged letting Jesus lead you. The second verse gave him credit for being a mighty good leader.

Funny, I learned that song when I was around nine years of age. Today; it still resonates in my soul fresh off the press. Even now, I still find my relationship with Christ as being refreshing and revitalizing as I continue my personal journey with Him.

I had a sneaky feeling Grandma and the other women of prayer weren't just mouthing some words, but they knew what they were singing about. I could readily see the seriousness in their eyes. They believed the very words they sang were true.

Not only could you sense their personal intent and commitment within the lyrics of that song, but the fragrance of their love and trust for God in uttering those words as they sang was evidence they knew Him well and trusted Him personally.

It was something about the way they expressed themselves in the words of that song. The lyrics flowed freely from their lips as their hearts were being consumed with pure praise and adoration for their King of Kings. I could tell they were acquainted with the person they sang about.

To Grandmother and her friends, their time spent in the presence of God was all that really mattered most. They made it a point to live in the moment, even when difficulties and challenging times threatened to consume their peace and interrupt their harmony.

The women held fast to their true convictions about God being their leader. They seemed to have no doubt where He was taking them in their personal journeys as well.

As a child, I was always so fascinated and intrigued by spending time around older women who had already travelled where I believed one day, by the grace and mercy of God, I too would travel. I would do just about anything in my power to eavesdrop as often as I could when they met. I wanted to take in all I could while it was before me.

While most kids my age would rather be outside playing sports, learning new cheers for the cheerleading team or forming some type of club, I spent a lot of my time, believe it or not, daydreaming and pretending I was being invited at the special table by the ladies to converse with them about the goings on in their lives. Yes, even at an early age, I began to dream bigger dreams and had outstanding expectations regarding them all.

Mature (older due to respect and not necessarily age) women in particular fascinated me because of their dialogue for one and their demeanor in other aspects. Even when young, you can tell a lot about a person by several methods, such as the tone of their voices, their facial expressions and their actions. It was quick to pick up on who worked the plan and who only talked about a plan with no true conviction.

The older women with wisdom tended to possess a special nurturing spirit about them. The majority of the time, they could be found always singing, smiling and releasing hearty laughter — the kind where tears streamed down their faces as they shared personal stories amongst themselves. They possessed something very special in their overall demeanor, and their daily walk always captured my attention.

They had a unique resilience and strong conviction that no matter what their personal challenges were, they always had an ace in the hole to which they could fall back on in the worst case scenario. They always talked about this man called Jesus as though He lived right next door.

When one of the women was downtrodden, the others were careful and quick to join in to lift their spirits through a "word of encouragement" or a soft reminder through a promise of scripture. Like a flower receiving a fresh drop of dew, I watched the women literally minister and raise each other's spirits.

Whenever they talked about their relationship with Christ, it was personal and surreal. I could see it in their eyes and hear it in their voices. No pretense, no doubt. God was very real to them, and He was near them at all times.

To these women, this God was not somewhere in the wild blue yonder. He was within a prayer's reach, a teardrop away, a moan or a lifting of the hands away. He was always near them.

I sensed in their personal times of trouble, trials and even during their times of tribulations, He was always around, taking them through, bringing them out and giving them the victory in all and overall. These women knew God loved them, and He was in fact Lord over their entire lives.

I witnessed on many occasions the women gather around their special table in the house. They would share their concerns with each other as it related to various issues such as money, of if one of the ladies did not have enough food to prepare for their families for the week or even the other necessities for that day. No one left emptied handed. This was accounted for both in deed and in prayers.

Special things—even peculiar things—happened within the gathering of the women during their intimate dialogue regarding their "Mighty good leader."

I used to sneak and hide so the ladies didn't know I was watching. I paid close attention to their conversation as they each shared what they called their "personal testimonies" about how well their leader showed up in their personal lives that week.

From the beginning of their meetings, one would start off by saying, "Child, it's been a little rough for me this morning. My husband didn't work much this week, but I talked with my Heavenly Father. And I told Him all about it. I don't know how it is all going to work out, but I just know He'll work it out for my good."

Within seconds, another woman would interject and say, "Child, He's a mighty good Leader."

They all would laugh and say, "Oh yes, He is."

By the time their weekly get-together was adjourned, none of those women left the same way they came. They seemed to have a pep in their steps and pride in their stride as they left their special gathering around the table in the house

It was as if they had some type of special code even during their conversations together. No one questioned what the other really meant. It appeared as though all who gathered around the table knew the code as well and was very familiar with the "Man upstairs" as they would sometimes call Him.

Somehow the women carried themselves as if this was not just a God over yonder somewhere over the horizons meeting. Rather, He was indeed Lord over everything, and they deemed Him as being Mighty in battle and more than able to do anything but fail. They trusted the Mighty good leader over their marriages, with their children, their finances and their health.

What I loved and admired about these special women were their tenacity to love and their willingness to be free in their vulnerability around each other. They didn't gather separately but as a unit. When each of them took their seat around the special table, they became unified in a spirit of oneness, and they looked out in prayer for each other's needs.

When they prayed they were careful to call out each other's needs and hold dear to each other's special request. When the prayer time was over, they were diligent in their response as their Mighty Good Leader had lead them to do so. In other words, they listened carefully to how they could each extend a helping hand in that requested need.

If any women at the table were wounded, no one felt free to leave the special table until the other's wounds were healed through prayer, sharing and caring. If one didn't have enough food for their household and children, those in the group shared what they had from their meager means. If one was short of funds, they didn't loan something. They shared their provisions such as they had, and the Lord added such as was needed.

In all of my years of watching the women at the table, I never saw one who came in broken, wounded, hungry, hurt, battered or bruised leave the table empty handed. At least they left different, mainly because you could always count on someone in the group saying, "Lord, you're a Mighty good leader," and you could count on the follow-up phrase being, "Yes, He is."

We don't just serve a God who is capable of doing something every now and then, but we indeed serve a generous, caring, all sufficient God. One that is Almighty in all of His ways. He is incapable of not blessing his people and loving us, because He is love. God always leads by example.

> *"But now, thus says the LORD, your Creator, Jacob, And He who formed you, O Israel, "Do not fear, for I have redeemed you; I have called you by name; you are Mine! When you pass through the waters, I will be with you; And through the rivers, they will not overflow you. When you walk through the fire, you will not be scorched, nor will the flame burn you. For I am the LORD your God.'"*
>
> Isaiah 43:1-3 (NASB)

XIII. AFTER YOU GO THROUGH, THERE'S NO WAY OUT BUT UP

Many times in life we experience setbacks, broken dreams, a bad marriage, the loss of a spouse or loved ones, bad career choices. Sometimes we feel life has not been kind to us. In those moments, we don't know how to continue the journey or who to turn to for help or answers while we are travelling in the journey. At times, we may feel alone and completely lost.

Sometimes the trauma and hurt that stems from it all can be too overwhelming and traumatic. It seems we can never recover or bounce back. At other times, we don't feel as though we have any reason to continue or the courage to try one more time. Unfortunately, we may quit entirely too soon.

Others simply may decide to just give up and throw in the towel because they don't see how they could possibly ever come through on the other side better than how they went in. They are ashamed, bewildered, and downtrodden and often times rejected, sometimes shunned by those who used to say they loved them.

Sadly, some may never recover from what they deem a personal devastation, embarrassment or loss in their lives, and they make a decision not to try any more.

There are times I believe in everyone's life—no matter how good we think we are, how educated we may be, how rich or well off we are, or for that matter, how long we've been married to the absolute love of our lives—pain will enter through invisible cracks we didn't know were exposed.

Often times, especially when we are not necessarily in tune and not paying attention to important details, if we are not mindful, suddenly life can swoop in and overpower us. Situations bring us to our knees with fear, doubts and trepidation that appear to be too much for us to survive through.

Pain has a way of causing us to question the very fiber of our existence even when we were so sure just a few years, months or even weeks ago about ourselves. Pain has a way of getting our attention one way or another—from one method or another means. Pain knows no boundaries or exempts anyone from its grip. And if there is one noted thing about pain, it is definitely not bias.

I am and have been very acquainted with such pain—unfortunately on too many hurtful and distressing occasions. Beginning in 2001 at the loss of my dad, then in 2003 my spouse had a heart attack in the same room where my father passed.

Later, in 2006 my spouse had his first stroke in Atlanta, Georgia while visiting his nephew. I remember getting a call from his doctor there on a Sunday afternoon just after I arrived home from an incredible church service. They informed me that I should hop on the next plane to Atlanta, where they would make him "comfortable" until I arrived.

I still remember the doctor's words that day, as I listened with disbelief over the phone.

"Mrs. Murphy, are you Audie's wife?" He didn't wait for an answer. "Ma'am, we have your husband here in our emergency room. He was just brought in with a massive stroke. His blood pressure is hovering around 278/100, and he is incoherent." The doctor paused for only a moment—long enough for me to utter some form of acknowledgement.

"We'll expect you to arrive later tonight?" It was more of a question than a statement. "We can make him comfortable until you get here."

With that, our conversation was disconnected. My entire body went numb, and all I could say was, "Jesus!"

Pain didn't stop there. It continued to loom around me. In 2008 after working on a job for exactly eight years, I was suddenly let go for no apparent reason and treated as though I did not matter for all the incredible years of service I provided the company. Not so much as a written note that said anything negative about my performance.

I was faithful in attendance, came in early, always stayed late and did more than my lion's share without being pushed or prodded. My middle name almost became "project," because I was always the one they could count on to head up projects and see them through. Yet, without hesitation, I was the first one they dismissed.

And then to completely finish me off, pain came at me with the big guns this time, fully intent to kill, steal and destroy. October 2011 my oldest brother died suddenly, November my spouse was laid off from a job following 18 years of diligence and service. Oh yeah he received a package and a note pretty much saying, "Thanks, it was nice knowing you."

In April 2012 the beloved rock of the family, our pillar that stood in the gap for all of us, our beloved mother's health began to deteriorate. Little by little, for me anyway, I became devastated and saddened by it all.

Still, in September of that same year, coming home from work, I couldn't reach my spouse by phone or text. I found him on the floor in the middle of having another severe massive stroke, unable to move and barely able to communicate.

As I continued to call his name and prayed at the same time, he looked up at me, reaching out his hand toward me and said, "I am alright baby, don't cry, I am alright."

At this point the pain was so deep, it literally stifled my own breathing.

This last bout of pain wasn't about to be finished. It reared its ugly head in the death of my sweet niece Sharon in March of 2014, and later that same month to be exact, I found a lump in my right breast. That was when they diagnosed me with breast cancer. I followed up by having foot surgery in September 2015.

Through it all, to the glory of God, while being in the very midst of everything, I can report without the least bit of hesitation. Our God is so big and so incredibly mighty, and His plans for our lives will always be victory! No matter how dark, bleak, hopeless, dysfunctional, uncaring the world and our trials may be or become, our God loves us unconditionally.

> *"But now, thus says the LORD, your Creator, O Jacob, And He who formed you, O Israel, "Do not fear, for I have redeemed you; I have called you by*

> *name; you are Mine! When you pass through the waters, I will be with you; And through the rivers, they will not overflow you. When you walk through the fire, you will not be scorched, nor will the flame burn you. For I am the LORD your God."*

Isaiah 43:1-3 (NASB)

This is one of the bases on which my strength and hope stood. During this entire process, I knew and fully understood I could not for one minute afford to look to the left or to the right. I clenched and held on to the thought that the only way I am going to make it out of this horrible, horrible pit is by looking directly up to God.

I learned how to lean, trust and totally rest in His true sovereignty. There were no other options or things that mattered most. I needed the presence of an Almighty, All Knowing, Powerful, and Wondrous Working God on my side. On my worst days I kept reciting Isaiah, inserting my name where needed.

> *"When you pass through the waters, I will be with you; And through the rivers, they will not overflow you. When you walk through the fire, you will not be scorched, nor will the flame burn you. For I am the LORD your God."*

I cannot speak for others, but during my times of real need, my entire focus was on the fact He alone was "Brenda's God." I didn't concern myself with what He meant to others.

Who else relied upon Him? Or for that matter did they

called on Him? All that mattered to me in those stressful moments was a simple request. "Lord, please go before me and make all of my crooked paths plain." And then I waited for Him to do so.

Though it has been a relentless and sometimes tedious process, God has been with me and my household every step of the journey, and He has indeed been very good to us on every leaning side.

In fact, if I really am truthful, He didn't just bring me along the way. He literally carried me and shouldered the load for me, because I was incapable of handling it for myself.

There were times during my trials and testing I thought I might lose my sanity. But this Amazing God would send His Word by way of the Holy Spirit to sooth my very fears. He'd tell me, "Brenda, the enemy is after your mind. You must guard it with your life."

He reminded me through His Word that He was the Good Shepherd, and I shall not want for NO thing.

He told me through His Word in Psalms 46:1-11 that He alone was all I needed, and I could rest in Him and depend upon Him for all my needs to be met. He even reminded me in verse 1, the word "refuge" in this instance meant He would be God for me when I found myself in a "tight spot."

> *"God is our refuge and strength, a very present help in trouble. Therefore will not we fear, though the earth be removed, and though the mountains be carried into the midst of the sea;*
> *Though the waters thereof roar and be troubled, though the mountains shake with the swelling thereof. Selah.*
> *There is a river, the streams whereof shall make*

glad the city of God, the holy place of the tabernacles of the most High. God is in the midst of her; she shall not be moved:
God shall help her and that right early. The heathen raged, the kingdoms were moved: he uttered his voice, the earth melted. The LORD of hosts is with us; the God of Jacob is our refuge. Selah.
Come; behold the works of the LORD, what desolations he hath made in the earth. He maketh wars to cease unto the end of the earth; he breaketh the bow, and cutteth the spear in sunder; he burneth the chariot in the fire.
Be still, and know that I am God: I will be exalted among the heathen; I will be exalted in the earth. The LORD of hosts is with us; the God of Jacob is our refuge. Selah." (KVJ)

After coming through all of the above mentioned circumstances with my faith and God's favor intact, I know my Redeemer still lives, and He is well able to do anything but fail.

Through my faith I have grown tremendously. My vision for outreach to aide and assist others to get to know the Lord has become clearer and more determined. My reason to praise Him has become more priceless.

SECTION FOUR

"And they overcame him by the blood of the Lamb, and by the word of their testimony; and they loved not their lives unto the death."

Revelation 12:11 (KJV)

XIV. WHEN YOUR TRIAL BECOMES YOUR GREATEST TEST-I-MONY

Our God has given each of us significant, precious and incredible gifts that far surpass any earthly gift we could ever dream or imagine. These gifts cannot be purchased in any retail store, commercialized market or via Internet services.

In fact, they are not man made and cannot be exchanged for any other item in the Heavenlies. These gifts are watched over and monitored by the Almighty God who sits high on His throne and looks low at the steps of all of His precious children. They are detailed in every manner.

When the conversation of temptation, testing and trials comes up, depending upon who is being asked the question regarding its definition, some people would say all testing or trials come from the Lord. However, according to 1 Corinthians 10:13 Paul said, *"And God is faithful; he will **not let you be tempted beyond what you can bear**. But when you are tempted, he will also provide a way **out** so that you can **stand up under it**."*

First let's examine the word "tempt." On the one hand, tempt could be looked upon as something that is considered to be "temporary," as a "fill-in" or "stand-in." Tempt could also be described as alluring, enticing, excitement or arousal. It also means "test or the act of being tested" in an unrestricted or limited manner.

In our day and time, however, the word temptation is more so used primarily as the making of a trial of a person being put to the test which can be demonstrated through various means and methods.

One of the most common methods known to us is someone who is being challenged through their health, circumstances, situations, career or general livelihood. Some of the reasoning for testing could be done for:

1. The benevolent purpose of proving or something specific
2. The malicious aim of showing one's weaknesses or trapping that individual into wrong action.

Whatever the reason, its purpose is to see what you, individually, are made of at the end of the day. Over the years, whether it is through my teaching exercises or just questions asked in general, it never failed, the subject matter of "Why does God allow" or "Why does God cause" trials and testing to come?

"These trials will show that your faith is genuine. It is being tested as fire tests and purifies gold." 1 Peter 1:7a (NLT)

Well, let's dig deeper, shall we, into how and why God tests Christians.

I believe God already knows exactly who I am. My strengths and my weaknesses, my limitations as well as my abilities, simply because it was Him who formed me and knitted me together in my mother's womb. So that fact alone takes all the guesswork out of my life already.

One of the primary reasons I believe God "allows"

testing through trials in our lives is because it is one of the most effective ways, methods and tools that can be used as a measurement for mankind. With testing we realize who or what primary source we turn to in the times of our troubles.

Secondly, who do we BELIEVE is able to deliver us while we are in the midst of our trials and our troubles? I believe God is not interested in me coming to Him in times when I think I am in trouble. The truth of the matter is, when am I not?

God desires for me to know He is the "Always, Ever Present, Never leave nor has He forsaken me" God every day. He is not just some emergency agent standing by waiting on me to think I might need Him. Neither does He want to be treated like He is my special errand boy on 24-hour call.

God is God, period. And He should be Lord over my all.

One of the ways we can readily see who we depend upon when we are in trouble and in general is based upon who or what we talk about the most while we are "going through" the trial or the testing. For example, if my constant conversation is on the "thing" or the matter at hand and not on the "deliverer" of the thing, I am not spiritually there yet.

If I magnify the problems more than I magnify the Name that is above every Name who is Lord of all, I am still not there yet spiritually. If I take the word of others who have no investment in my overall well-being more so than I am willing to seek ye first the Kingdom of God and all of His righteousness, I am still not there yet.

So I believe our God tests His people by allowing the error or the situation we find ourselves in to reveal first and foremost to ourselves the quality and sincerity of our faith and our devotion unto Him. Then we can see what is in our hearts.

God allows the trial to be His method of purifying the believer as metal is purified in the refiner's crucible. He uses the measurement of what we believe He is able to do for us before, during and even before the trial and testing have subsided.

I am always amazed whenever I watch the evening news, which I do not do often. However, when I do, and the meteorologist relating the news states something along the lines of, "About 170 reports of wind damage have been received in a swath from southeast Oklahoma, eastward across the Mississippi Valley, Ohio Valley and Tennessee Valley, to as far north as southeastern Lower Michigan between 7 a.m. EST Wednesday and 7 a.m. EST Thursday.

"The most significant wind-damage was in Sharp County, Arkansas, where several homes were reportedly destroyed. There have been multiple reports of large hail, mainly from eastern Arkansas into Kentucky, which have caused some damage to vehicles..."

Even going to such lengths as asking the public to stay off the roads due to flooding waters on roadways in low-crossing areas. Yet even armed with this plea and visible barricades in tow, there will still be those who choose their way instead and override common sense or proof that tragic things will and often do happen when evidence is not followed through.

When trouble inevitably follows suit, the first thing these individuals do is call upon the very authority they ignored in the first place to bail them out of trouble. They will have the audacity to become angry when help didn't arrive fast enough.

This is sometimes the same stance we take with God. We get into trouble, then call upon Him, and He bails us out over and over again. However, at some point, sometimes our own doing brings about the trials in our lives. At other times trials or testing are of no particular fault of our own. Nevertheless; they do take place.

And when this occurs, I believe our God will use those trying times to strengthen us through our dependence upon Him. If we will allow the process of that particular trail to run its course in the Name of Jesus to take place believing God has a plan for our outcome, He can use it.

Other times, if allowed while in the trial, our patience can mature to its perfect work through our faith in God. For a lot of baby Christians, that is a source and potential for spiritual maturity — especially in their Christian character as He leads them into an enhanced assurance of His love for them. Through faithfulness in times of trial, men become "approved" in God's sight.

There are so many Christians who still believe Satan has some type of control over their daily lives, and therefore, he is making or causing these trials to take place. Many think they do not have any control, authority or power over their situation.

But, yes we do. We can open our mouths and speak God's truth over that situation and walk out the victory through faith and belief in God.

While I believe Satan does have a role in some aspects of trials and tribulations, he does not have control. Some, if not most of the time, we inadvertently relinquish that right ourselves. Satan only can use what is appropriated to him by ourselves. For instance, if we are thoroughly convinced God loves us, the devil will say He does not because of a sinful act we may have done. And because we are not 100% confident God loves us unconditionally, we fall for the lie every single time. All the while, Satan goes prancing around with our victory in tow.

I think when we give entirely too much time, attention and mediation to our problems and circumstances, and less time communicating with God about our thankfulness and gratitude to Him for being Lord over everything, we fall prey to the enemy's games and his lies that God doesn't care about us, and He is somehow disappointed in us.

The enemy will try to convince us God will even perhaps turn His back on us and our situations while we are in the middle of troubles. With this mindset and attitude, it is very easy to give up and to give into the devil's lies, which causes us to be defeated and overtaken.

Satan will always test the people of God as long as there is breath in our bodies. According to Discipleship Defined, "He tests God's people by manipulating circumstances, within the limits that God allows him, in an attempt to make them desert God's will.

Christians must constantly be watchful and active against the devil, for he is always at work trying to make us fall. There are four main schemes that Satan uses to succeed in the destruction of Christians:

1. He tries to crush us under the weight of hardship or pain.
2. He tries to urge us toward a wrong fulfillment of natural desires.
3. He tries to make us complacent, careless and self-assertive.
4. He tries to misrepresent God to us and create false ideas of

His truth and His will. Matthew 4:5 demonstrates Satan can even quote (and misapply) Scripture for this purpose.

What has been a major catalyst for me in my various storms in life has been one of three deliberate steps:

1. Keeping accurate records through journaling major events that have happened to me during and after my personal storms. By using this method of keeping track, it has allowed me to go back days, weeks and even years later after the aftermath to review His track record in delivering me out and bringing me through those situations. I seriously take to heart if He did it once, He can do it again.

2. I am mindful to ask God to allow me to see the particular lessons I am to learn while being held up by the storm. The desire for me is not grumbling about the testing or the strength of the storm per se, but the life lessons to be learned while in the eye of it.

3. I want to learn, grow, and rest while in the storm. Understanding the strength of the storm is being solely controlled by the Maker of all things helps me recognize from the beginning of the storm to its end, God has expiration timing for it all.

4. No matter how challenging and difficult the storm is with all its raging winds, and violent rain, God still has a pulse and an expiration date on it all. He will not allow my feet to slip or permit me to be overtaken in the midst of it all as long as my focus remains on Him.

I personally never thought I would live to say this, but I am truly grateful for my storms. They have indeed helped to shape the various fibers of my destiny. Through each of them, I believe I have emerged out of them triumphant and more victorious.

Admittedly, at the time, I didn't necessarily welcome them or for that matter, even want them to ever take place. But once involved, I realized Greater resides on the inside of me. When I thought I was at my weakest, God showed me I could indeed endure and weather the storm because of His

Living in Purpose

great grace and mercy at the forefront.

Because of that, I knew I was being freshly renewed daily every morning. The love of God was enough to sustain and support me throughout any of life's torrential rain storms. While in my storms, I learned how to acknowledge Him as my Divine Protector!

Some of my trials showed up at the most inopportune times while other storms appeared to be too stubborn to leave. Yet, at the Name of Jesus, no matter what, they had to go and never return. Some of my trials came to challenge my faith, and others merely came along to disturb my peace and rob me of my joy.

Unfortunately, there were times when I didn't know the magnitude of the power of the Name of Jesus that was extended to me through my personal experience of being born again. I unknowingly allowed my temporary storm to get the upper hand by letting my guard down for others to take full advantage of the situation.

I thank God that even while being in my personal storms, God was with me every step of the way. He alone allowed His gracious hand to rest upon my life and the life of my beloved family.

He didn't allow me to drown, suffer needlessly, to be overtaken, used or abused. He was Lord over all. Thank you Jesus! I have and still am amazed at the magnitude of power in the Name of Jesus that was provided to and through me during the magnitude of my personal storm.

> *"Be strong and courageous. Do not be afraid or terrified because of them, for the LORD your God goes with you; he will never leave you nor forsake you."*
>
> Deuteronomy 31:6 (NIV)

Trials are considered formal examinations of evidence before a judge, and typically before a jury, in order to decide guilt in a case of criminal or civil proceedings. It is also a test of the performance, qualities, or suitability of someone or something. Additionally, a trial can be viewed as being the testing of a person, thing, or situation that tests a person's endurance or forbearance.

In referencing our trials, we must not overlook Scripture or think it is strange when we enter into our trials and tribulations. According to the writer of Hebrews, we will all have our fair share in time.

> *"And have you forgotten the exhortation that addresses you as sons? My son, do not regard lightly the discipline of the Lord, nor be weary when reproved by him. For the Lord disciplines the one he loves, and chastises every son whom he receives. It is for discipline that you have to endure. God is treating you as sons. For what son is there whom his father does not discipline?"*
>
> Hebrews 12:5-7 (ESV)

In the New Testament, the Greek word for trial means "to prove by testing an event that demonstrates the genuineness of your faith in Christ and refines the quality of your spiritual life."

So let's come to an agreement on this definition: A trial is a painful circumstance allowed by God to change my conduct and my character. Therefore, my conduct—is considered what I do. And to a deeper level, my character then becomes who I am.

Most of the time, it is safe to say we believe we know ourselves very well outside of pressures and various stresses. But when a little unexpected, undue pressures comes and hangs around for a lengthy amount of time and challenges the very fiber of our being, or when the true testing of our character is really exposed, unfortunately it is not always revealed in the best of light under those conditions.

Our trials can be viewed as the way God is fine-tuning us, if you will, in our actions we choose in that moment to react, respond or deal with a particular situation.

Most likely, those moments in which we choose our behavior in responding or reacting to the stresses or pressures happening to us or within us, God will use them to assess our character that can be used as a tool to guide us in ways more beneficial to kingdom building moving forward.

There are several Biblical terms for trials that can be looked upon as interchangeable: suffering, hardship, tribulation, chastising, and discipline. Let's face it. Trials are hard times no matter what. And I do not personally know of anyone that wants to endure them — not even for the slightest moment.

Nothing about trials, in my humble opinion, is cute, spiritually deep or should be exalted. Trials are indeed hard and can sometimes appear unbearable.

These hard times vary both in intensity and duration. When I look back over my life, for as long as I can remember, there were very few warnings about my personal trials and tribulations. I just opened my arms with a bright smile on my face and simple welcome.

For the most part, the tribulations in my life took me by storm unexpectedly. When they happened, they were fast and furious, altering my life forever in that manner and specific season in my life. Not one storm or trial left my life intact as I knew it. When the storm was over, that particular moment in my life was finished as well.

I was left with new direction, new territory, new beginnings and interestingly enough a new outlook on life itself. It is very important to know and fully embrace that a trial can stretch over months or years, or in some instances, decades. A trial can be small and irritating or huge and shattering.

The one thing we know for sure about trials is everyone experiences them. There are absolutely no discrepancies at all. Your zip code cannot shield you. Your neighborhood won't exempt you. Dropping what you deem as important names from powerful worldly figures won't protect you. Rich, poor or middle income cannot bribe the storm in our lives, because trials know no boundaries or exceptions.

Life happens to all of us sooner or later. And the more mindful of that knowledge the better prepared we can be when the actual storm lands at our zip codes.

The real truth of the matter, if while reading this book you are a child of the Most High God, you are indeed either going through a storm, coming out of the storm or soon to be in the middle of a new storm.

There is no way around them. Storms of life are inevitable, and they happen to each and every one of us. You need to know, not everyone's storm is designed alike. Some people survive them while others succumb to them. The overall choice is left up to us in the end.

Not only are our storms different, they vary by our faith, tolerances, strength, belief and endurances. Storms also are varied in sizes, shapes and forms.

Have you ever wondered how someone else's storm

may appear to be astronomical and virtually impossible for them to endure? You might think to yourself, "How in the world is that person going to survive or make it through this?" While others can break a shoe heel and almost go ballistic behind it because it was a "designer" shoe?

God knows each of our strengths and our weaknesses. That's not all. He also knows our faith and trust levels in Him as well. God knows for all mankind when facing trails and difficulties in our lives, it is the most difficult aspect of life's journey.

It really doesn't matter what type of storm, the endurance level of the storms or whether the scale ranges of the storm varies from 1 or 10. What matters most is where our faith, hope and trust lies while being entrapped by the storms.

You see, the storms could be physical, relational or economic. It does not matter whether the storms are emotional or circumstantial. A storm is a storm is a storm, and they all hurt and wound us in the aftermath of our lives.

Another very important factor about storms in life is there is no guarantee your storms will come in single file. On many occasions, I can personally testify, storms sometimes come into our lives in what I call "clusters."

Meaning one day the car can break down and there is an unexpected very expensive price tag that comes along with it. You don't have the money saved up to take care of it. And the next day you discover you need gas in the car, and your credit card is maxed out.

Not only do you not have a rainy day account, you have not seen the rain in that account for several months— possibly even years. In fact, the rain has been missing for so long from that account; it can be respectfully listed as a "drought account." And as soon as you get that bill paid and the car repaired, what you know, the air conditioning is going out.

So then, where do we begin in our healing process of the aftermath of our storms? Well, let's take a sneak preview into Hebrews 12:5-7 as it relates to gaining some insight about what are trials.

As we revisit this same passage of scripture reading again, let's look for other clues. The subject is discipline, a term that describes God's involvement in the hardest part of our life. The definition for discipline can be viewed as the suppression of base desires, and is usually understood to be synonymous with restraint according to Bing Dictionary.

Discipline is considered as training. Training no one enjoys or likes at the outset. It's like parental instruction very few, if any, can really value and appreciate—at least not until after maturity.

It is only when the babies have matured and often times moved out on their own and experienced life a little for themselves. Then they can really value and genuinely appreciate the true meaning of discipline once given by a loving and wise parent who knows what's best for their child and sees the benefit from certain discomfort and pain. A child's desires are no guide for healthy growth.

Growing up, my mother would say to me (right before the discipline began), "Brenda, this is going to hurt Momma more than you."

Every time, I thought to myself, "Yeah right, sure it is. If you are going to feel that way about it, how about just skipping the so-called discipline altogether?"

Well, I don't have to tell you the ending to that story.

Often when my mother completed the discipline she would say to me, "Bren, I love you and I am only trying to spare you from life's pain down the road. You cannot do everything you see your friends do because you are not their child, and I am responsible for your upbringing and how I shape your life."

Overlooking my part in the processing of being disobedience that in some ways created the outcome of what caused the root cause of my "discipline," I didn't in the moment accept her idea of saying she loved me. My view was distorted.

At the time, I choose to interpret her discipline as being meanness and revengeful and not love at all, because she didn't see things my way. And she certainly wasn't having any of my ready-made excuses I had already conjured up.

So likewise, some of us are like that today when God discipline us because of our own disobedience. Though he takes care of us before, during and after, we do not want to receive His words of love to us. We are too busy pouting and being content with embracing our emotions to focus and or receive His discipline as any possibility of love.

When God says, "I love you, and that is why I am allowing you to go through this test. It is not to break you, harm you or abuse you, but rather, this is what will bring the best out of you for the next phase of your purposed journey,"

We can believe His words during discipline are the truth.

When He saved us back at Calvary over 2,000 years ago, He started the process He will continue until the day we die. Salvation is just the beginning.

Trials mean God is working on us and through us. We will continue to see occasional discipline in our lives down here on earth until He returns for us. And when His work's done, it's Heaven for you!

Test the waters right now by writing the answers to the

two questions below:

- What are the trials in your life right now?
- How would you describe the lessons you've learned about God so far in these trials?

Next, seriously pray over those responses, and expect God to provide the answers to your concerns and heart-felt prayer.

Prayer: *Heavenly Father, thank You for not holding me accountable for enjoying or liking my trials or trying to appear super-spiritual while they are present in my life.*

Thank You even more for teaching me You can provide joy to me while I am in my trials. Thank You for the hope in You that remains in spite of trials when I purposefully place my focus on the Name that is above my every trial.

Forgive me for times when I slip into self-pity or doubt about Your faithfulness towards me. I thank You for allowing me to take a moment of reflection about those things You alone have brought me through successfully, which is enough to remind me You always have been faithful to me in all things. As I reflect, my mind turns what I consider a deeply distasteful trial into a sweet memory of Your closeness. So I thank You for all this in Jesus' name, Amen.

> "Lord, please teach me to trust Your will for my life, especially when I cannot feel your presence surrounding me."
>
> — Brenda Murphy

XV. ALL THINGS ARE WORKING FOR MY GOOD

"And we know that all things work together for good to them that love God, to them who are the called according to his purpose. For whom he did foreknow, he also did predestinate to be conformed to the image of his Son, that he might be the firstborn among many brethren. Moreover whom he did predestinate, them he also called: and whom he called, them he also justified: and whom he justified, them he also glorified. What shall we then say to these things? If God be for us, who can be against us? He that spared not his own Son, but delivered him up for us all, how shall he not with him also freely give us all things?"

Romans 8:28-32 (KJV)

"For our light and momentary troubles are achieving for us an eternal glory that far outweighs them all; So we fix our eyes not on what is seen, but on what is unseen, since what is seen is temporary, but what is unseen is eternal."

2 Corinthians 4:17-18 (NIV)

XVI. THIS TOO SHALL PASS

While the phrase "this too shall pass" is misquoted as a Bible verse, it is not in the Bible at all. However, it does bear in some ways a close proximity to another Scripture reference located in 2 Corinthians 4:17-18 which talks about our troubles being "light and momentary."

During those hardship moments, we should not focus on our troubles, but rather we should *"fix our eyes not on what is seen, but on what is unseen."* As we continue to trust God to keep us and bring us through our trials, this too shall pass.

That is a great way to look at our trials and testing, no matter how strenuous and tumultuous they may appear. This too really is going to pass, and we do not have to believe or think they will necessarily end in doom and gloom or not in our favor. God indeed has a blessing with our name on it.

Often when life throws us a curve ball, it is somewhat a very surreal and natural instinct to believe or readily think of the worst case scenario as opposed to being optimistic at the outset until we learn further about the situation.

When most people receive bad news, they temporarily pass out for lack of oxygen. Then when they recover and find out the news wasn't as grave as they originally expected, they bounce back and say, "I knew God would bring me through it all along."

As we grow in Christ, I do believe He wants us to search for Him and long to spend quality and necessary time alone with Him to really get to know Him in a relational manner. As we choose to spend amply time with our Heavenly Father, we will find it is not always about "correction" or our asking Him to work out a problem or a situation on our behalf. We can also receive "revelation" and preparation for the next level of fellowship and restoration in Him.

The more quality time I spend in the presence of God I realize it's the "knowing" Him that makes all the difference in the world. The more I get to know Him in a "relationship" manner, the more at ease and dependent I can come to rest in Him.

That's important to me, because I don't want to call on Him only when I am in what I call a "panic-stricken" moment or times when I deem them to be 'hardships.' I really want to go deeper in my understanding and building a relationship with him.

As I meditate on the Scripture reference *"For our light and momentary troubles are achieving for us an eternal glory that far outweighs them all,"* those words put me in remembrance of the fact that although, to us, our trials seem at times unbearable or insurmountable to handle or to deal with, they are nothing our God cannot handle.

The good news is for one, we shouldn't be handling our trials on our own in the first place. God is more than able to handle our problems. If we allow Him to, they can become what I refer to as "shared interest." Meaning, I cannot just drop them off at His feet, keep moving and never learn anything from the experience. Learning from trials keeps me from continuously repeating the same cycle over and over again.

Secondly, God refers to our moments of afflictions as being light and "momentary" at best. The word momentary means very brief, lasting but a moment. My favorite one is "fleeting," which in my opinion means, not anything worthy of too much attention. It's here today and gone in an instance.

How can the Bible make such a statement? Because God truly knows the order of our lives, and He alone stands in total control of it all. Though we live in His will, we also have the ability to ask and strive to live in His perfect timing and receive the expressed assurance no good thing will He withhold from us that love Him.

We never have to live one moment in fear God is out to get us, control us, and harm us or make us suffer. God is love, and all He does for us is out of His love for us. His name and His actions are one. They are impossible to become separated. God's name alone isn't just love, but He is love—pure and simple.

I am growing each day in my walk with the Lord, learning the more I "fix my eyes on what is seen," I began to sink in utter despair. Allowing a temporary portal to develop where fear, doubt, worry, stress, and even a spirit of being overwhelmed tries frantically to make its abode in my mind, which causes my reaction to the temporary situation around me.

By focusing on the temporary situation happening in my life at that present moment, I was not recognizing I magnified the problem to a point where it was so out of control. It almost overrode what I know the Word of God has spoken about that particular instance in the first place.

At that time, I came to the conclusion if not careful, I allowed the things I meditated and focused on to become larger in my mind, creating a negative outcome of exactly what I was calling in over my life.

Not understanding how focusing on such negativity can bring about those sinking reactions caused by a sense of overwhelmness and hopelessness into fruition over time. I didn't fully grasp the thought that whatever I had been giving my strength and attention to would one day manifest into my reality — whether I was ready or not.

Over time I began to pay more attention to my thought patterns, especially those specific thoughts that always seemed to rain on my parade out of the blue or at least without warning. I must admit that now, I am more conscious of making every attempt to pay closer attention to what I am thinking about and meditating upon, because I want my thoughts to give birth to positive things and things that inspire, encourage, motivate me for the greater good.

I am careful to declare and decree those negative things are under my feet and are defeated. They no longer have dominion over me because of the blood of Jesus Christ who paid it all for me. Now, I call into my life those things that are good, lovely and pure. Those things that bring me joy and allow me to share that joy with others.

"What I feared has come upon me; what I dreaded has happened to me." Job 3:25 (NIV)

It is really vital that we as children of God start to think about what we are thinking about the most. Our words are "power based" and our words will inevitably breed into our lives what we are talking about and believe — even if it's for a fleeting moment.

Sometimes a negative thing can occur in our lives so

quickly we respond and/or react without ever thinking about what we said and continue to speak over our lives.

Whether we are incognizant of what we are speaking into our lives does not change the fact we are still calling those negative things in, intentional or not. It is up to each of us to "make time" and deliberate effort to hold ourselves to what we say and think on a daily basis and do the necessary work for change and improvement along the way.

I understand it can appear to be a very daunting and difficult challenge to change the way we see, hear, respond or react to life incidents. Unfortunately, this is a "self-improving" class we all have to take if we want to move forward through the much-needed transformation stages to take place in our lives for the betterment.

> *"So we fix our eyes not on what is seen, but on what is unseen, since what is seen is temporary, but what is unseen is eternal."*
>
> 2 Cor. 4:18 (NIV)

This is a deliberate and intentional stance we take for ourselves. After all, in order to do better, we must desire better in every way. We can't allow ourselves to wallow in the worst case scenario and hope for the very best as a natural outcome. It is not going to happen. Deliberate thought and effort must be provided at the forefront of change.

My personal understanding of the phrase "fix our eyes" is to rightfully and appropriately engage my time, energy, attention and effort to something important and worthy of my consideration. To gaze at without disturbance or interruption. Fix to me means to enjoy and immerse myself in the thing that has my undivided attention.

So to fix our eyes is to focus all of our energy on what really matters most as to not allow ourselves to become emotionally, physically or otherwise detached from that which brings us joy, solace, peace and energy.

I am a believer of the Word of God, and I believe the promises He made to me are true, yes and amen. Therefore, I fully engage the fact that, based on our history together and my past experiences of His manifold blessings, I have no doubt I can rest in His assurance whether the thing I am hoping for has been manifested yet or not. My hope in the fact of who has spoken the promise over my life is enough to hold my attention until it shows up.

I have learned about myself that unless I believe the Word of God and His promises for myself, I will not get excited or expect anything from my "fixing" my eyes on the thing I am hoping for until it is finally revealed and in the end is not faith. That is simply doubt dressed up and presented in a different box.

I believe the true relief from "This too shall pass" does not happen once the event or the circumstances in my life have ceased. Rather, I am trusting God during every step of the way while in the midst of the storm's pathway. It's my reflection and the direction I am taking while the storm is wreaking havoc in my life for the world to see and to take note of.

How I respond to the "this too shall pass" as it relates to my attitude and disposition while the storm remains shows me whether my trust and confidence is truly in God or in myself and my surroundings. My knowing and personal stance in God will allow me to tunnel through safely onto the other side, being assured He is more than able to lead, guide and direct the storm for my good no matter how long it remains.

"The important thing to me is that I'm not driven by people's praise, and I'm not slowed down by people's criticism. I'm just trying to work at the highest level I can."

Russell Crowe

"But I will hope continually, and will yet praise thee more and more."

Psalms 71:14 (KJV)

XVII. A YET PRAISE!

Psalms 71:14 is my sentiments exactly. As long as I live, I will forever continuously hope in Christ my Lord and Savior for all things concerning my life, family, ministry, salvation, joy, peace, hope, love—the list is endless. I recognize Him every single day of my precious life. He alone is the Head, Source and the Resource of my existence.

I recognize without Him, Brenda Murphy cannot do anything at all. Not some things, absolutely nothing. Whether it's considered valuable or not, I cannot even raise my arm without His supernatural strength. I cannot advance in my healing unless He heals my body and provides me with His anointing to do so. I cannot assist in any advancement of Kingdom building unless He opens the right doors, provides the provisions, the directions, the wisdom and guidance in and over my life.

Without His purpose, plan, provision and anointing upon my life, I could not do anything at all to bring honor to Kingdom building. I am grateful for Him as being the soul force and driving power of my entire being. I am fueled, infused and energized by His Word and His promises over my life. I am so thankful I know Him personally, and I have His favor upon my life.

Not only am I favored in his pavilions, but daily I know I have an open dialogue as well as an open door through which I can come boldly before His throne. There I find refuge and a safe haven for all of my ills.

I will never have to suffer backlash for entering in too much or too early, because He who watches over me will not suffer my foot to be moved. I echo the sentiments of David in the 23rd Psalm that He is the Good Shepherd over my life, and I shall want for absolutely nothing.

I will never have to worry about safety because He never sleeps nor does He slumber. He alone watches over me day and night. I choose to believe He covers me under Almighty wings. Not only does He keep Israel, but He is more than able to keep me as well.

I am thankful He is forever mindful of my every need. I am reminded in Psalm 23, He is the Shepherd that places me a "green" pasture, where my life will be forever restored, and my soul is always refreshed so I cannot dwell in the spirit of lack. Therefore, I shall not want for anything.

When I truly think about the goodness of Jesus over my life, and I meditate upon my life being forever in His care and plan, I am carried away by what that means to me today. Just the mere idea of I am forever His and He is forever mine is mind boggling.

Think about it.

Someone who has absolutely nothing to offer an Almighty, All knowing amazing God, has the potential to gain everything through the acceptance of the blood shedding of Jesus Christ on the cross at Calvary years ago. This thought is almost incomprehensible. Our minds cannot easily grasp this truth.

The acceptance of Him into my life means I can never slip through the cracks of being out of His perfect will for me, because He holds me in the palm of His hands and His perfect will. I fully embrace that today I am the righteousness of Him because of His Great Name!

Daily I am being fortified with the knowledge no weapon of any kind that rises up against me "shall ever prosper." No, it cannot win. Jesus has assured me through His Word I need not take any thought about tomorrow. For my tomorrow will take care of itself. The gracious arm of the Lord is resting upon me. I can count upon Him for direction, because He goes before me to make my crooked paths plain.

I thank God my yet praise is not contingent upon my future circumstances, situations or lifestyle. My praises unto God are not predicated upon the bases of whether the world loves, accepts or even receives me. When I welcome the fact that God loves me, that's enough. Even while writing this book, the Lord is causing great and mighty manifestations to take place in my life.

Through the Word of God, I am one of the official beneficiaries of His unsurmountable blessings, breakthroughs, miracles and favor in my life. Daily, the pages of God's Word makes my life bearable, possible, and it provides for me the ability to stand strong in His will. Through His Word, I choose to believe new doors are opening and breakthroughs are being released — openings I could previously only dream or imagine about years ago.

The more I am learning to relinquish my trust and confidence unto the Lord, the more I am becoming aware of Him planting my feet on solid ground. I have fresh understand that He is causing His biblical truths to be established in me daily.

As I learn to live for Christ, the more I am aware his presence and provisions are connected in and around me. Sitting quietly before the Lord and having the patience and willingness to rest in his presence causes me to become more sensitive to His existence. All is well indeed.

One of the many reasons I live in a constant "yet praise" is because I serve a "consistent" God. Now, more than ever before, I am coming to know I cannot allow my emotions, thoughts, old patterns, feelings and circumstances to become the driving forces of my mood for worship or failure to worship. Sometimes the best praise happens when I am in the midst of my temporary hardships and trials.

Instead of trying to wait until the moment of sadness, fear, doubt or "weariness" passes, I am learning to praise Him in the midst. My praise flows because of who He is and the mere fact He is not moved or changed at all regardless of my temporary circumstances.

He is a gracious, kind, merciful, Almighty, unlimited, mindful, truthful, exceedingly, abundant, and everlasting God. He is Lord of Lord and Kings of Kings. Through Him, I am able to live above my needs and not crushed by the sheer semi-strength of them. I am able to be the head and not the tail, the lender and not always the borrower — even when my financial means don't always line up as they should.

Not only is He consistent but He is also a "concerned" God. He cares about His sheep, for He instructs us through His Word to be cautious of things and pay attention to our surroundings, so as not to become easy prey for our enemies to devour us at a moment's notice.

Ephesians 5:15-27 encourages us.

"Look carefully then how you walk, not as unwise but as wise, making the best use of the time, because the days are evil. Therefore do not be foolish, but understand what the will of the Lord is." (ESV)

The Lord wants us to make thoughtful decisions that bring glory to His name and will bless the people we encounter. The Kingdom of God is vital to Him and it should be to us as well. Winning souls for the Kingdom is a big undertaking. As Christians, our number one goal in life is to please our Father in what matters most.

With that being said, it is imperative we pay close attention to how we carry ourselves before God and our fellow man, being mindful of how we communicate and interact with others who are saved or otherwise. We should not redeem our time here on earth casually as though the Lord is not soon to come, nor taking into account we are expected to work while it is day. When the night comes, no man can continue to work.

The beauty of it all, is I can have a yet praise because God left no stone unturned. He gives us to know we should not be deceived into thinking every spirit is the same, and He said so in 1 John 4:3. *"Beloved, do not believe every spirit, but test the spirits to see whether they are from God, for many false prophets have gone out into the world."* (ESV)

This means we must continue to pray and seek the face of God for wisdom and direction, lest we ourselves be fooled and carried away. Not only must we seek the wisdom but we should also carry out the very principal of that wisdom in our very own life.

One of the most successful tools the enemy continues using to keep the wool pulled over most people's eyes, including some Christian's, is simply the more "busy" we are, the more some feel they are accomplishing greater things for the Kingdom of God. That is not necessarily accurate.

A yet praise to me translates into being available to hear from God and to respond according to His will for our lives. A yet praise is taking God at His word and carrying on the business of the servanthood of Kingdom building and being a blessing to others at the same time.

A yet praiser is represented and motivated by doing the will and purpose of God with the understanding and belief God alone is in total control over it all. It is God alone who extends to the believer the opportunity to try the Word of God for ourselves and to prove and permit God to do what He has said He would do.

In other words, I don't have to wait until I see victory to know I am already victorious in the things He promised me. All I have to do is choose to release my faith and belief God has already done the work. Then I must walk in my God-given authority to lay hold to what he already said for my life.

A yet praise, to me, means there is more in store for me—a greater outcome for my situation, circumstances and my future, if I only believe it to be possible. I need not rush, get in a hurry, and become frustrated or live in despair because He who began a good work in me is more than able to complete it through His plans for my life and my personal journey.

In my personal praise, I do not have to thrash around in agony and despair nor allow the devil to beat me up with negativity and unimportant chatter about my past. I recognize Jesus loves me. He cares for me and He calls me his own. Because of His grace and mercies shown toward me, I can move forward in His perfect will and purpose for my life.

My yet praise lets me know I can be happy even while being in the midst of a private storm. I know, according to Isaiah 43:2-3, *"But now, thus says the LORD, your Creator, O Jacob, And He who formed you, O Israel, 'Do not fear, for I have redeemed you; I have called you by name; you are Mine! When you pass through the waters, I will be with you; And through the rivers, they will not overflow you. When you walk through the fire, you will not be scorched, nor will the flame burn you. For I am the LORD your God, The Holy One of Israel, your Savior; I have given Egypt as your ransom, Cush and Sheba in your place.'"* (KJV)

The more you praise and celebrate your life, the more there is in life to celebrate.
~Oprah Winfrey

"But because you are not My sheep, you refuse to believe. My sheep listen to My voice; I know them, and they follow Me. I give them eternal life, and they will never perish. No one can snatch them out of My hand."

John 10:26-28 (BSB)

XVIII. YOU SHOULD NOT FOLLOW WHO YOU DON'T KNOW

I have never been more assured about anything in my life than I am right now. I am utterly convinced as a born-again believer in the Name of Jesus Christ I cannot afford to allow myself to be deceived in thinking there is anything or anyone greater than God.

It doesn't matter to me how difficult, challenging, trying or horribly wrong things may appear to be in the world or in my life today. I know our God is real. I fully acknowledge God alone is the absolute keeper, Shepherd and Lover of my soul. He is more than enough, all sufficient and the Greater in my entire being.

He is the Alpha and the Omega of my life. The entire foundation of my faith, hope, dreams and desires are predicated upon the Name of Jesus alone. In fact, His very name is a constant presence in my mouth. Not because I am trying to impress others but rather because He has been just that good to me and my entire family. I just cannot tell it all!

I know for sure today in a world full of turmoil, confusion and shortcuts, the only way we can make it and be remotely sustained is by the hand of God and the leading of an Almighty Savior. He is more than qualified to keep us from falling.

I am a living witness our God can be counted on to pick us up and place us back on the path of His righteousness no matter how far off the track we have gotten. God knows all, sees all and can do all. For me, there is no other name greater.

I tremor to think how I could even exist without the presence of God in my daily living. How could I survive without His hand resting upon my life? Just look around today and see how many unnatural things are taking place within our society, culture and world. Consider how people in leadership rolls are calling things politically correct, which by God's Word are blatantly wrong.

I am somewhat shocked we are living in a time where the President of the United States is openly disrespected merely for his skin color alone. Yet we have those individuals who reflect everything but a true leader's integrity, skillset morals or mindset that are being hailed as potential great leaders of our time.

When I look at the potential candidates that could quite possibly become our world leaders, it makes me want to live on my knees consistently before God. I'm asking for grace and mercy to continue to surely follow us and lead us in the right direction for our nation, our homes and our families and friends.

Whether we are ready for it or not, whether we are asleep both spiritually and mentally at the wheel, our nation, family and our very lives are in trouble. It has just gotten this way, but it has been in this mode for quite some time.

The candidates we have before us now who are considering and running for presidency are more concerned with discrediting each other. They try to make the other individual look bad, showing very little evidence of their "real intentions" if voted into the position.

Not only are they all promising all kinds of corrupt ideas and broken promises prior to taking office, each of them truly expect the citizens of this nation to govern ourselves accordingly. They seem to believe we will adhere to their blatant abominations at will.

God is and has been calling for His people to come to the forefront and be accounted for. He says in John 10:27-28, *"My sheep listen to My voice; I know them, and they follow Me. I give them eternal life..."* (NIV) So whether or not we think it matters, it really does matter who or whom we choose to follow as it relates to our lives and choosing the correct paths.

Why you may ask? Well, because our very lives and our livelihoods depend upon it. Clearly in the word of God He continues to say in John 10:28, *"... and they will never perish. No one can snatch them out of My hand."*

God is not speaking of only for the moment. He is talking about for eternity. When we choose to follow God, it is not just so we can make right decisions or be told right from wrong.

We choose to follow Him because our destinies and purpose are tied to His will for our lives. We should not be so eager to attach ourselves to anything that has a "similarity" of God's favor but isn't real.

God is not hot today with love for us, but by sundown tomorrow, He is unsure or unaware of the goings on in our lives. He is intimately aware of our every move. He has great expectations and plans for our lives both here on earth and in heaven. Even though some may not think of purpose as being a big deal, it is more important than we think.

Living in Purpose

Recently, I was preparing for our spring conference and there was a particular segment featured with individuals either in business or starting a business I had hand-selected to be a part of the event. While each of the ladies agreed to participate, they understood the particular requirements and expectations required of them.

In the 12th hour of the preparations, I received a phone call inquiry from a person I didn't know who wanted to know about the possibility of being a "vendor." When I returned the call back to the gentleman our conversation went something like this.

"So, are you the leader of this event?"

"Yes, I am."

"Are you Brenda?"

"Yes, that's me."

"Well, I just want to come and sell my stuff? How do I do that?"

Once I got over the initial shock of it all, I inquired about more information from him. I wanted his name to begin with and how he heard about the conference.

After a few questions and minimal dialogue from him, I asked if he would be interested in "attending" the conference or just "selling his stuff?

"Well, I might be" he said. "I mean I just want to sell my stuff. I've got t-shirts, socks, caps, pants…"

And on and on the list went. He was absolutely clueless and oblivious to what the intentions of the conference were. I believe, he didn't much care.

I believed it absolutely never crossed his mind about whether what he was asking was in decency and in order. The only thing he cared about was himself and how he could make money at the expense of me. Or whether he was even a good fit for the conference.

He didn't ask any questions of me at all about the entire event. All he wanted to do was get in at the last minute and simply "sell his stuff" at my expense, of course. He wasn't concerned about the intent of the conference, but only wanted to make some money for himself.

Sad, but true. This is for the most part how some of us treat our relationship, or the lack thereof, with Jesus. We have no intention of following Him or adhering to His expectations about His will for our lives. We just want the mega blessings that someone told us about through preaching, teaching or maybe through the luck of the draw. Then we can appear real spiritual and appear prosperous to the general public at large.

I am convinced many of us suffer needlessly at the hands of those who don't understand, nor can they accept our worth and value. They will spend countless hours, effort and useless energy trying to sabotage what they may perceived as a façade when it is really our God-given and ordained "purpose" that cannot be broken, slighted, hindered or forgotten.

The cost of pursuing God for our purpose is absolutely, unequivocally priceless. Look carefully at what He says in the last few lines of John 10:28, "...*I give them eternal life, and they will never perish. No one can snatch them out of My hand.*" (NIV)

All I can say at this point is Jesus! What a mighty good Leader we have in Him. He not only promises to lead us and keep us, but the verse ends by saying, "I will give those who are willing to follow Me eternal life and they will never PERISH. No one can snatch them out of My hand." Glory be unto God.

What an ultimate guarantee no other politician, friend, foe, enemy, prince, chief or anyone else can guarantee or promise. God is not the exception. He is the Rule and the Ruler over everything.

When we choose to follow God, we benefit tremendously from His leadership. First and foremost, we have His assurance of peace when we allow our minds to be stayed upon Him. Also, whatever we are facing in life, the Word of God provides us with uncompromised confidence we will get to the other side of it—if we will just remain focused on Him.

With our desire to please Him and follow His leadership, we have His assurance. When we allow Him to become our ultimate refuge in the times of difficulty and challenges, we have a God who will fight every battle—if we would just choose to remain still.

We have His promise. He will never, ever leave us when the world becomes cold and heartless. We can depend upon our God for everything. No matter what.

> "Do not despise these small beginnings, for the LORD rejoices to see the work begin, to see the plumb line in Zerubbabel's hand."

> Zechariah 4:10 (NLT)

XIX. A FINAL NOTE REGARDING PURPOSE

I am so very thankful to Jesus Christ, my Lord and Savior on so many levels. He desires for me to always come to Him and ask for wisdom whenever there is a void of wisdom and understanding.

Now I grasp the fact I need not wander around aimlessly trying to figure things out or work them out on my own. Now I know all I need to do is go to God's word for wisdom and clarity.

> "If you need wisdom, ask our generous God, and he will give it to you. He will not rebuke you for asking."
>
> James 1:5 KJV

We do not have to ever wander around in stressful situations of confusion, too proud in our own strength or possessing a haughty spirit that will not allow us to simply inquire of our Heavenly Father. He has the right answers or direction we need to move forward, especially when we do not know which direction to take for our lives.

God is more than willing and able to lead, guide and direct us from the very beginning to the eternal ends of our journey—if we are only more than willing to ask, receive and then follow His instructions.

God desires to know us in a personal and intimate manner and He wants nothing more than for us to really get to know Him, and then to lean on Him for all things.

The mere thought we were created in Him shows us a lot about the heart of God and His thoughts toward mankind. More importantly His thoughts toward us as his sons and daughters. He would never desire for us to struggle or be wary about what He has for us, especially when all we have to do is ask.

We never have to rely upon others' thoughts, opinions, criticism or feelings towards us, because God's views of our lives are the only thing that ultimately matters. We should never be willing to place our livelihood, image of who we are or our very purpose in the hands of any person. That is too hefty of a price to pay for their responses. Besides, the only opinion that should resonate with us at the end of the day is God's.

As it relates to purpose, I associate the same with our "identities." Since we were formed by God, it seems befitting to me we should return to Him without any questions or concerns we have about who we are and whose we are. Simply put, "everything" originated with Him. At the end of the day, or lives are too precious to put guesswork in it.

It saddens me when I find there are many individuals in the world today turning to others and asking, "Who Am I?" While there may be those who can help nudge or guide someone in the right direction, the most safe and best place to start looking for answers, clarity, assurance and truth is in the Word of God. Our true identities are not hidden "out-there" in space somewhere, known only to a few prominent people or those with specific degrees and certificates.

It is a very scary, scary thing to rely on or relinquish all of our confidence into the hands of any man to describe our true worth and identities. God knows the unaltered plans for each of our lives, and even when things don't appear to be working out or turning out for our good or seemingly for our favor, God is never confused or at a loss of words concerning our outcome.

With man, for the most part, sometimes ALL we can see is "right now." And most, if not, all of what we see is just the commonality of what is presented before us. Man has a tendency to count every flaw whether it's before, during or after. Man can and most often is very quick to remind us of where we've come from and not where we are headed.

How often we have failed. And if we are not careful, someone may even speak their version of what we will not be able to accomplish. All they can see is what's right before their very eyes. But our loving God sees and knows beyond our tomorrow. At the end of the day, He's the One my real focus must be on.

No other person on this earth can possibly detail out our lives according to their "limited understanding" and even more skewed perception of the true plans God has for our lives. There are those individuals who feel as though our past will forever dictate our future, and they can come up with a better road map for our lives than what our God already meted out—at least in their minds.

Please be forewarned. There is just no way it can be done. Other people are just like you and me, limited in our own ways and our own understanding. Without the wisdom, guidance, discernment and direction from God, there is no way our times (as related to our lives) will ever rest in the hands of another human being.

And besides, our individual fate is far too great to be placed in the hands of someone who at best just knows what they see on the outside of our hearts and flesh. I say trust the One who created us from absolutely nothing and placed all He is within us to navigate our entire lives from start to finish.

It is not a very good idea to inquire about our identities from others who do not have our very best interest at heart. At best, it is a very dangerous idea to rely upon or even consider the opinions and thoughts of others as they attempt to define life on our behalf. No one else has the power or real ability to discern accurately our true identities nor to genuinely ascertain in what aspect God will use our gifts for His glory. There is just too much at stake.

There are so many opportunities for this very important information to become misconstrued and wrongly interpreted by others for our lives. So why should we even attempt to lay such a major decision at the feet of someone else who is incapable of fully knowing or understanding what God has planned for our lives?

If there is one thing I have learned on my personal journey, whatever God wants me to know, one of the surest ways of making sure I receive it is through His Word and prayer. The other means is through meditation and fasting. God has a way of letting us know what He alone has to say about everything that concerns us. He doesn't need anyone's help to do so.

And while there are different approachable avenues of receiving the answers we need by way of God, in the end, the confirmation will always be found in and through His Word. If what is being told to me, regardless of the method it may arrive, does not line up with the Word of God, it should be rejected at the outset. God's Word will never contradict His promise or His plan.

The Bible is very, very clear. If we "lack" wisdom, we can "ask of Him." *"If any of you lack wisdom, let him ask of God, that giveth to all men liberally, and upbraideth not; and it shall be given him."* James 1:5 (KJV)

In this scripture, we can readily see the exactness mentioned about the precise method in which God wants us to know unerringly what our identities are in Him. He does not want us depending upon mankind to relay, guess, and gesture or provide assumptions about who we are to God as it relates to the Kingdom or about whose we are.

As a people of God, it is our duty to desire of Him what is His good and perfect will for our lives. As a believer, I want to know the wisdom of God for my life in order to be able to observe through His sovereignty His will for my life and that of my family.

I want nothing but His perfect will to be manifested in my daily walk, talk and my entire being. Daily I strive to continue learning how to be still and know He is God, who does all things well and wisely concerning me.

Day-to-day while unraveling the mere fact He is more than just one entity helps keep me grounded. Recognizing I can find anything I need from Him in His word or through prayer and even in focusing my attention on what's good and pure.

Some days, just a simple song of my personal adoration unto Him goes a long way. I love the fact my relationship with Him is so personalized and intimate.

Because I consider myself to be a private person being able to have a one-on-one relationship with an ALMIGHTY God is beyond my earthly comprehension. The mere fact He loves me so much He desires to commune with someone of my lowly demeanor amazes me. This thought makes me want to be a better person in general. It gives me something greater than myself I can strive to ascertain through Christ Jesus.

I am grateful I know it is in Him I live, move and have my perfect being. Being armed with that revelation makes me want to draw nearer to Him and choose to remain hidden under His wings. Knowing I can choose to have everyday dialogue with Him floods my heart with joy unspeakable.

Not only can I commune with Him, but He also responds to my heart desires with godly wisdom and direction. Some days, I just long to be in His presence and ask nothing but to be near Him. That's enough for me. The more I seek Him, the more of Him I become on various levels.

Today, I am beginning to understand I will never know or understand it all until I am home with Him, actually in His glorious presence. Still, it is intriguing getting to know and consistently growing in Him daily. I am honored that even while being a private person, my discussions with Him are not only personal but are priceless as well.

I enjoy the fact I can share my entire heart, soul and mind with Him, and He accepts, informs, guides, instructs and corrects me without rejecting me all at the same time. I enjoy the fact that every time I am in His presence, I am always comforted because I step away with more than I entered in with.

I love the fact He approves of me even when I am disappointed in myself. He never condemns my brokenness or my imperfections. He never says, "I told you so" or looks away from my woundedness. But rather, He always encourages me through my mishaps and mess-ups and He never overlooks my efforts no matter how minuscule they are.

He sees me as being relevant, useful, and beneficial to His Kingdom building, and He constantly affirms my desire to please and live out His will for my life. Even in my efforts and greatest intentions to live out His perfect will for my life, I feel Him near me, cheering me on to move forward within the plan. It makes me feel good that I matter to Him in the Kingdom of God.

I can respect to some degree the various concentrations, disciplines and efforts it takes to become a part of certain fraternities, clubs and memberships. While they hold such disciplinary, grade-point averages and status quo to a certain level of standard in order to become a part of such a group, there is absolutely none grander than being part of the army of the Lord where the requirements are trust, obedience, humility and a sincere desire to please Him.

There is nothing more vital than knowing our names have been entered into the Lamb's Book of God for eternity. He alone has accepted us just as we are. What an awesome privilege that is. I cannot fathom anyone not wanting to be a part of such a journey and experience.

Our God is so amazing! He has invited each of us to become a part of His royal family forever. Imagine being a part of such a dynamic, everlasting, empowering, peace that surpasses our understanding. Through the blood of Jesus, we have become a part of a Kingdom where there is no more sickness, death, depravity, or suffering of any kind.

We have inherited a place where there will be no more killing, no rejection, no poverty and no negative stigma at all. We will forever "live" in the present of an Almighty loving, caring and able God. I cannot speak for anyone else, but just being able to sit in the presence of an all-knowing, purposeful God who is nothing but love—this is simply beyond amazing.

When I think of purpose, I cannot help but associate it with peace and serenity. Because unless and until I understand the role I have been placed on earth to accomplish through my life, I realize I cannot fully grow and appreciate my true reasons for being.

Purpose to me is about extending myself beyond what I "think" I can do to "evolving" into what I know I can become through the power and leading of a gracious God. He is more than willing and capable of ordering my steps to assist me in birthing that manifestation of His will for my life.

Purpose is that driven, innate, persistence that contends with our conscious until we say yes to the perseverance that keeps us grounded to the cause at hand. Purpose is love at its finest. It is the acceptance of everything beautiful and magnificent our God alone has created within us.

God was so committed to the purpose for our lives, He was specific about every part of our being when He created us in His own image. He was so dedicated to having a real relationship with us through eternity, He didn't leave it all up to chance. He sent His only Son in our stead.

> *"For God so loved the world that He gave His only begotten Son, that whoever believes in Him shall not perish, but have eternal life. For God did not send the Son into the world to judge the world, but that the world might be saved through Him."*
>
> John 3:16-17 (NASB)

One of my favorite quotes from Dr. Martin Luther King

is:

"The ultimate measure of a man is not where he stands in moments of comfort and convenience, but where he stands at times of challenge and controversy.

Faith is taking the first step even when you don't see the whole staircase.

Our lives begin to end the day we become silent about things that matter."

After reading Dr. King's quote, I thought about another very important word that came to mind as it relates to purpose and that is "courage." It takes an amazing amount of courage in today's world to walk out the God-driven purpose He has for our lives. It is not enough just to seek God for the purpose. It also takes great discipline and focus to walk it out.

We must be reminded the devil and his imps will try everything within their limited power to try to detain, delay, and deter us from reaching our greatest potential for the Kingdom of God.

If they cannot defeat us one way, they will try relentlessly another way. But thanks be to our Lord and Savior and through the blood of Jesus, we are more than a conqueror to finish strong and have been assured by God, we already have the victory through our sonship in Jesus Christ.

> *"Nay, in all these things we are more than conquerors through him that loved us. For I am persuaded, that neither death, nor life, nor angels, nor principalities, nor powers, nor things present, nor things to come, nor height, nor depth, nor any other creature, shall be able to separate us from the love of God, which is in Christ Jesus our Lord."*
>
> Romans 8:37-39 (KJV)

I am glad God Himself created our identities and established our true worth and value in Him. In today's society, unfortunately, if you do not know for yourself who you are in Christ and whom you serve, if that door is open to chance, practically anyone could deceive you through outlining their personal opinions and ideas of what it looks like.

Let's face it, even the Bible declares that everyone that calls upon the name of the Lord does not mean they ever really knew Him.

> *"Many will say to me in that day, Lord, Lord, have we not prophesied in thy name? And in thy name have cast out devils? And in thy name done many wonderful works?"*
>
> Matthew7:22 (KJV)

It is sad to say that even in some churches today, some are bold enough to stand in the position of a leader and declare they have a "Word of Knowledge" from the Lord concerning our purpose—only to collect a "nominal" fee for their efforts by way of a "seed" in harvest.

Over the past three to six months, I remember being pursued by one person in particular who relentlessly sent me mail concerning my future that supposedly only he knew. All this even though he had never met me nor heard of me. For that matter, he didn't really know for sure I even existed. Yet he felt it necessary to request I send a certain amount of funds by a certain date, to a certain address. For my "faith-efforts," I would receive a prayer cloth, or a bottle of water, with instructions about how to put the item on a specific windowsill in my home for a prescribed amount of days. Of course, I could get this entire wonderful prize for the low, low cost of just $27.15.

My heart really aches for those who really desire to know Jesus in a sincere way. They are looking for answers and "true leaders" who are authentic and genuine, who will not dress up as wolves in sheep apparel, rent church space and fleece the people of God just because.

As a follower of Christ, we must do our part in choosing to read, study and pray on our own and to seek the Lord about His purpose in and for our lives. We must stop relying upon others to write out our destinies on our behalf without our input, feedback or consensus.

Today, more than ever, we need to seek God's face first and foremost before making a single move. We cannot and must not even remotely attempt to become wise in our own eyesight as it is written in Proverbs 3:6-8. We must learn how to completely trust and rest in God.

> *"In all your ways acknowledge Him, and He will make your paths straight. Do not be wise in your own eyes; Fear the LORD and turn away from evil. It will be healing to your body and refreshment to your bones."*
>
> Proverbs 3:6-8 (NASB)

I believe it must grieve the heart of God when He sees His children looking for our true identities in our self-righteous purpose. We are constantly grasping for bigger edifices, self-promotion, more need to be seen rather than understood as it relates to the purpose of God and helping others to recognize God as being the head of the church. This identity comes our mere flesh.

In today's society, the church services are becoming shorter and the commercialism surrounding the church seems to be advancing more and more. I never thought I would see and live in a day where more preachers, pastors and leaders are proclaiming God has given them a great vision to build a specific type of ministry. However, there is very limited fruit to see otherwise.

Sometimes, there is such a great need in the local body of believers that gets severely overlooked, unmet and sometimes simply dismissed altogether due to a conglomerate of reasons or excuses.

I do know there are certain guidelines and even restrictions that must be followed, even in the local church. However, more discernment should be followed in making decisions rather than relying on feelings and emotions.

It is unfortunate the local churches are sometimes filled with those individuals who have been in church for most of their lives but have never been taught or fully understood the most basic discipleship from Bible teaching.

Daily I encounter someone who references more about what their parents used to say or do as it relates to church and very little about what the Bible says. Often they can't cite any examples used in the Word of God. While it does not make this person a bad or unlearned individual, it does make them vulnerable. We must learn how to stand on the Word of God for ourselves and not on what others may have told us, or for that matter what we think or feel about the situation. God wants us to know who He is personally. He desires a personal, unique relationship with each of his children.

I strongly believe when the local church and body of Christ makes a personal investment in those who attend their church, the world will see and know a resounding difference for all. And when charity of the love of God begins at home, as it relates to demonstrating the true love of

God, the local body at large will be blessed and healed.

I believe every member should be equipped in the house of the Lord. There should be no deficiencies or insufficiencies as it relates to men and women knowing what God requires of each person in a daily walk with Him.

If the local church chooses not to make an investment in the body, the church will continue to suffer and remain on milk. Before long, it will become stagnant and unable to function as it should.

What I mean by that is the church, meaning people, not being able to equip the saints who are attending the local church. They must first understand the importance of grasping and learning about the importance of discipleship within the local body of Christ. We must understand what it means to assist others within the local body before launching out into the deep, trying to assist and build up those in foreign countries.

I am definitely not saying foreign countries do not need the local churches' love and support, both financially and through other means. However, I do mean a lot of local churches not only suffer for lack of knowledge, wisdom, and continuity, but also with supplies. And once again, I do sincerely believe charity always, always begins at home first.

Naturally this doesn't apply to all churches, pastors, preachers or leaders in general. Yet, we must not become too wise in our own understanding and eyes but rather diligently seek the Lord for a greater understanding in how we should proceed in this venture—regardless of whether it appears beneficial and godly.

We must become cautious about everything in the earth today. Our enemy is actively planting seeds of discord wherever there is potential for seed to take root. The enemy is actively looking to recruit any planters that will willingly accept his despicable seed into their hearts and allow it to germinate.

You may have noticed, like I have, that in today's time, it would appear it does not take long now for that proverbial seed to be planted and grow at records of lightning speed into the hearts of mankind. Therein the seed sprouts up relentless discord, anger, anxiousness and downright hatred—sometimes even death of friendships and possibly costs human life.

As prayer warriors, we must be diligent in our approach before the throne of the Almighty God in inquiring about His will for our lives and the lives of others. We cannot afford to lean unto our own personalized understanding about anything. It is vital to get an understanding from the Word of God about where we stand in the building up of the Kingdom each and every day. We cannot afford to keep putting off today what is needed and needful for tomorrow's generation.

No one is exempt in that movement. We are all purchased by the Son of God for a priceless sum. Jesus shed His blood for all of mankind. No one was left out or forgotten at the cross. Therefore, we owe it all to the Purchaser who stood in the gap concerning our souls.

And I strongly believe it is beyond time for every man, woman or child who professes to be a born-again believer to pay it forward. How? By living out loud the lifestyle of a born-again believer through our faith, trust, hope and joy of the Lord before others so they can see Him through our living.

All lives matter. There is no creed, color, race, classification or origin left out. Jesus died on that cross for everyone because He is love and His nature is love. And we all have a right to that tree of life both here on earth and beyond.

There are absolutely no exceptions to that promise. But there are some who have never heard of this freedom that cannot be obtained through any other method than the Name of Jesus. If we don't lead people to Christ by our living and obedience unto God, they will never, ever know He paid the price for them at Calvary.

Those of us in the body of Christ must wake up from our long slumber and ask the Holy Spirit to revive and renew our spirit in Christ once again. We must thirst and hunger after that which only the true and living water can replenish for our souls. We must look at everyone as a potential Kingdom builder — from the very youngest to the old.

We must become involved and concerned about our world's condition and stop allowing ourselves to become victimized by the sheer illusion of one man or woman's idea of what is right or wrong in his or her eyes. We must rise up and take possession of our true heritage and God-given authority to make intelligent decisions for ourselves based upon the Word of God and for the sake of our universe.

We cannot pass the buck on to others and try to hold someone else accountable for what our individual roles and responsibilities are in the world today. God is expecting something specific He alone has placed in each of us to carry out. There are no short cuts.

> *"So we aspire to please Him, whether we are here in this body or away from it. For we must all appear before the judgment seat of Christ, that each one may receive his due for the things done in the body, whether good or bad. Therefore, since we know what it means to fear the Lord, we try to persuade men. What we are is clear to God, and I*

hope it is clear to your conscience as well."
2 Corinthians 5:9-11 (BSB)

Each day we are given another opportunity to be alive in the earth should be spent with only one true agenda. And that is to please our Heavenly Father. We should thank Him for the many wonderful, breathtaking blessings He provides for us daily. Every day He loads us down with brand new mercies and blessings we cannot even comprehend. His mercies are fresh and new every single day.

I am so very thankful for the purpose God has placed in my life. I am thankful for the insatiable appetite that drives me to know His Word each day. To know His Word is to know Him. And to know Him causes every fear, doubt and question about His covenant with me to disintegrate in the presence of doubt.

God is a good Shepherd, and He does not want me to worry, stress and doubt His love for me. He is a caring, loving and thoughtful God who leads me, guides me and takes splendid care of me and every single need I have without fail.

Daily I find there is absolutely no searching of His mindset towards me. He desires for me and my family to prosper and be in good health. He has a plan for our finances and our overall well-being.

Knowing this, the more I study and learn about God, the more drawn to Him I become. The Word of God helps me abandon my fears, doubts, and reasons for being afraid. The Bible inspires me to throw caution to the wind and decide to move forward.

In drawing nearer to Him, I am becoming less intimidated by my current circumstances. I'm less afraid of what my critics might say or less nervous about the possibility of failure concerning tomorrow.

In fact, today, more than ever, I am more confident and assured the very One who holds my today, most definitely is more than able and capable of holding my tomorrow and even the times afterward.

"The mere possession of a vision is not the same as living it, nor can we encourage others with it if we do not, ourselves, understand and follow its truths. The pattern of the Great Spirit is over us all, but if we follow our own spirits from within, our pattern becomes clearer. For centuries, others have sought their visions. They prepare themselves, so that if the Creator desires them to know their life's purpose, then a vision would be revealed. To be blessed with visions is not enough...we must live them!"
- High Eagle

Purpose + Chance = Opportunity to do something great in this life no one else can do but you. Purpose to me means being deliberately set aside to do a work only you were created by the Almighty God to perform at maximum level and ability.

We were all created to accomplish that "particular thing" God has assigned each of us to complete. Purpose has to do with a set time in the earth's atmosphere to accomplish, achieve, finish and undertake what you were created to perform with the ability given to us by God alone.

Purpose is uniquely designed, carved out of our inner man the abilities, capabilities, skillsets, gifts and aptitudes to complete the task assigned to us before we were created and introduced into this world. We were created ideally with a specific person in mind. Our purpose cannot be duplicated, copied, transposed or transferred over to someone else to handle. It is instinctively meted out with great thought and design.

To make sure we were able to carry out this specific purpose within us, God never left it up to chance or happenstance. He knew the plans and what order our lives would evolve. He knew right down to every little bitsy detail the when, how and even the what. There are no details about our journey God does not already know about. That is how intimate our relationship with Him is. There are no mistakes, defects or misconceptions with God.

He is in the details. The very fibers of our everyday living expresses that. Even before the plan was set in motion and expected to be carried out, I believe a specific conversation occurred over each soul. Then, and only then, it was set free to come into the earth. In fact, one of my favorite scriptures in the Bible says it this way:

> *"For I know the plans I have for you," declares the LORD, "plans to prosper you and not to harm you, plans to give you hope and a future."*
>
> Jeremiah 29:11 (NIV)

In closing, let's choose to pay attention to what's up ahead. Live on purpose and be excited about the unlimited possibilities where our personal journeys take us. And always, always expect that something great is going to happen to you today, tomorrow and always.

Brenda

REFERENCES

www.thefreedictionary.com/crowd (definition of crowd)
www.HelpGuide.org
Rebekah Eklund, "Jesus' Teaching and the Crowds", n.p. [cited 24 Dec 2015].
www.bibleodyssey.org/en/people/related-articles/jesus-teaching-and-the-crowds
www.biblestudytools.com/dictionaries/bakers-evangelical-dictionary/comfort.html
www.Got Questions?.org
www.americanexpress.com/us/small-business/openforum/articles/top-10-attributes-of-successful-strategic-plans/
www.biblegateway.com/passage/?search=Revelation+12%3A11&version=KJV
www.discipleshipdefined.com/resources/temptation-and-testing
www.jarofhopes.com
Read more at:
www.brainyquote.com/quotes/keywords/praise.html#dPWgsvLQBBczBTQ3.99

ABOUT THE AUTHOR

Brenda is the Founder of Innovative Ministries, Inc., and the author and publisher of four books. Brenda writes from personal experiences and her daily walk with God.

Known for her spiritual wit, depth, and down-to-earth style, Brenda weaves colorful illustrations and some humor alongside biblical truth to help audiences find contentment, assuredness and endurance with the Lord. Through Brenda's signature wit and poignant story-telling, audiences are prompted to look beyond their circumstances and life situations to embrace, explore and receive the experiences of God's wonderful grace and mercy in the midst of adversity.

In her personal life and through her intimate walk with Christ, Brenda is discovering that every new day is a glorious fresh gift from God our heavenly Father to live in God-ordained purpose! Brenda truly believes that as sons and daughters of the Most High God, we can be confident, courageous and self-reliant in the fact that Jesus Christ, our Lord loves us beyond our human comprehension and to prove it; we only need to read the Word of God for ourselves and believe in Him alone to find out just how much He really cares about everything that concerns us.

Brenda Murphy is a captivating and inspirational Christian author and popular conference speaker. She has conducted countless women's conferences and has been invited to speak extensively as a keynote speaker both locally and abroad.

Brenda has served as worship leader, intercessory prayer leader, Sunday school superintendent, counsellor, and life coach, as well as a host for family-life conferences, women's retreats, mother-and-daughter brunches, and single events.

Brenda uniquely weaves her life story and her powerful teaching to create a message of encouragement, hope, and motivation to all. A message that challenges everyone to keep their eyes focused on the real prize, and that is none other than Jesus Christ who is Lord over everything.

Brenda is happily married to the absolute love of her life, Audie, for thirty-four years and she enjoys resting in the perfect will, purpose, and plan of God for their lives. Currently Brenda and Audie reside in the inspiring city of Fort Worth, Texas, which they proudly call home.

OTHER BOOKS PUBLISHED BY BRENDA MURPHY

- *Had It Not Been For the Lord on Her Side*
- *Raw Faith*
- *Forgetting Former Things: The Power of Letting Go*

www.ingramcontent.com/pod-product-compliance
Lightning Source LLC
Chambersburg PA
CBHW062216080426
42734CB00010B/1915